Mental Disabilities
and the
Americans
with
Disabilities Act

Mental Disabilities and the Americans with Disabilities Act

A Concise Compliance Manual for Executives

JOHN F. FIELDER

QUORUM BOOKS
Westport, Connecticut • London

Library of Congress Cataloging-in-Publication Data

Fielder, John F.
    Mental disabilities and the Americans with Disabilities Act : a
concise compliance manual for executives / John F. Fielder.
        p. cm.
    Includes bibliographical references and index.
    ISBN 0–89930–826–0 (alk. paper)
    1. Mentally handicapped—Employment—Law and legislation—United
States. 2. Discrimination against the handicapped—Law and
legislation—United States. I. Title.
KF3469.F53   1994
346.7301'3—dc20   93–42762
[347.30613]

British Library Cataloguing in Publication Data is available.

Library of Congress Catalog Card Number: 93–42762
ISBN: 0–89930–826–0

First published in 1994

Quorum Books, 88 Post Road West, Westport, CT 06881
An imprint of Greenwood Publishing Group, Inc.

Printed in the United States of America

♾™

The paper used in this book complies with the
Permanent Paper Standard issued by the National
Information Standards Organization (Z39.48–1984).

10 9 8 7 6 5 4 3 2 1

Copyright Acknowledgments

The author and publisher gratefully acknowledge permission to reproduce the
following:

International Classification of Impairments, Disabilities, and Handicaps, Geneva, World
Health Organization, 1980, pp. 47–67, 143–153.

The ICD-10 Classification of Mental and Behavioural Disorders. Clinical descriptions
and diagnostic guidelines, Geneva, World Health Organization, 1992, pp. 22–40.

"DSM-II-R Classification: Axes I & II Categories and Codes" from American
Psychiatric Association: Diagnostic and Statistical Manual of Mental Disorders, Third
Edition, Revised, Washington, DC. American Psychiatric Association, 1987.

Contents

Preface

Businesses with federal contracts have been legally required to make reasonable accommodations for people with mental disabilities since the Rehabilitation Act of 1973. However, the evidence shows that few have actively made an effort to do so. Why this is so is not fully understood, but probably has something to do in part with the continuing persistence of negative attitudes about hiring people with past or current psychological problems. It has long been known that employers' attitudes and hiring practices have generally not been positive toward people with mental disorders (Farina & Felner, 1973; Combs & Omvig, 1986). To expect a rapid reversal of workplace discrimination because of a legal mandate is therefore highly unrealistic.

The Americans with Disabilities Act of 1990 (ADA) has been in effect since January 1992. The law has widened already available protection against discrimination and covers many more Americans in the workplace. While businesses in general have complied with the physical disabilities part of the law, few have yet to develop and implement proactive plans to handle requests for accommodations from employees or prospective employees with mental disabilities. While this is due in part to negative attitudes, the law came with few interpretive guidelines for accommodating people with psychological problems and unfortunately does not require development and implementation of a plan. Moreover, many businesses believe that compliance will be expensive, even though it is either inexpensive or free to offer reasonable accommodations for most mental disabilities.

The category of mental illness has accounted for 9.8 percent of the first 11,500 discrimination claims filed with the Equal Employment Opportunity Commission (EEOC) since ADA went into effect. An additional 2.4 percent of the total claims were for alcoholism (Yandrick, 1993). The majority of these disputes have been settled out of court because most employers have been willing to make a good faith effort to resolve complaints constructively with the EEOC. As of July 1993, only 700 right-to-sue letters had been granted to employees alleging discrimination. What the future holds in terms of volume and resolution of cases remains to be seen.

Acknowledgments

There are many people who either directly or indirectly share the credit for this book. Those to whom I owe special thanks include attorneys John H. Feldmann III and Maria C. Brandt of the national labor management law firm Proskauer Rose Goetz & Mendelsohn for contributing the chapters outlining the Americans with Disabilities Act and the case law pertinent to mental disabilities under ADA.

Drs. Marilyn R. Margiotti and Daniel O. Taube of the California Institute of Psychology were especially supportive of this project and helped me work through some of the difficult problems that ADA presents for the mental health professions.

Ms. Maryann Zaremska, chief librarian at St. Francis Hospital, has been invaluable for her assistance in retrieving many of the articles used in this book.

Many thanks are due to my wife Julie and my son David for their tolerance and support. Julie in particular contributed greatly by reading the many versions of the manuscript and made many helpful suggestions about both substance and style.

Mental Disabilities
and the
Americans
with
Disabilities Act

Introduction

The Americans with Disabilities Act of 1990 (ADA) is generally viewed as the most significant antidiscrimination law since the Civil Rights Act of 1964. The framers of ADA followed the lead of the Rehabilitation Act of 1973 by offering protection to people with mental as well as physical disabilities. In particular, the statute prohibits discrimination in the workplace against workers with past, current, or perceived mental conditions who, with or without special accommodations, are able to perform the essential functions of their jobs. However, the ADA has been viewed as vague legislation. This is especially true for the mental disabilities part of the law, where guidelines are virtually nonexistent. The rationale given for the lack of guidance is weak.

In a joint analysis of the law, the U.S. Equal Employment Opportunity Commission (EEOC) and the U.S. Department of Justice arrived at the following conclusion regarding which physical and mental impairments are covered by ADA: "It is not possible to include a list of all the specific conditions, contagious and non-contagious diseases, or infections that would constitute physical or mental impair-

ments because of the difficulty of ensuring a comprehensive
list, particularly in light of the fact that other conditions or
disorders may be identified in the future" (U.S. EEOC & U.S.
Department of Justice, 1991). While this statement is true, it
ignores the fact that groups such as the World Health Organization (WHO) and the American Psychiatric Association (APA) have developed classification systems of mental
disorders that could and should serve as data bases for ADA.
The *International Classification of Impairments, Disabilities, and
Handicaps* (WHO, 1976) is probably the most sophisticated
and complete classification system of impairments, disorders, and handicaps yet constructed, and its existence
should have at least been noted in the ADA since it can
provide a valuable source of information for anyone who
is attempting to deal with an accommodation for a person
with a mental disorder.

The framers of the Rehabilitation Act and ADA also did
not use current medical nomenclature, nor did they provide
guidelines for how an employer should go about evaluating
a mental disability claim. ADA reads as if employee requests
for accommodations should be accepted at face value, when
this should never be the case. Also not addressed is who
should make a disability determination. For example, in
other disability systems such as workers' compensation or
social security, qualified examiners such as psychologists or
psychiatrists are designated to make a determination of
whether or not a disability exists and to what degree. This
is not mentioned in ADA, and some employers have been
left with the mistaken impression that it is up to them to act
in the role of qualified examiners.

In addition to these problems, ADA may also unwittingly
perpetuate a destructive myth. When applied to mental
problems, the words "impairment," "disabled," and "handicapped" have commonsense meanings for the public that
are generally associated with physical problems. One of
these meanings has to do with the idea of permanence. This

is one of the primary differences between physical and mental disabilities. While there are mental problems that are long-standing or permanent, those that do not have genetic or physical causes can often be altered when treatment is available and circumstances permit, and people with developmental disorders such as mental retardation may benefit from special education and training.

Mental health professionals have seen how destructive the mentally disabled label has been to many psychologically injured workers who have gone through the workers' compensation system. Many of these people have been terminated from treatment when examiners pronounced that further psychotherapy would not be helpful and that an injured worker was "permanent and stable." This has generally been followed by insurance companies discontinuing payment for psychotherapy even when the treating doctors and patients had evidence that treatment was successfully bringing about improvement.

Also, it is well known that when workers are certified as "permanently disabled," the chance for a psychological recovery decreases dramatically for many of them (Volle, 1975). This is one of the more tragic aspects of current disability systems. Going through this experience can be far more destructive than the original injuries because these people are often led to believe that they truly are permanently disabled, and this then becomes a way of life. The belief may also be reinforced by the additional benefits that are often gained by being declared ill. This is tragic because the individual incurs a disability in the sense that he or she may have lost any motivation to change. Another example of this is a welfare system that rewards people for staying unemployed by paying them more money than they can earn.

In addition, many of the very people who are covered by the mental part of ADA are offended by the terms "disabled" and "handicapped," which, they feel, convey erroneous

perceptions to the public. Members of Stomp Out Stigma
(SOS), for example, believe that the continued use of these
terms can only perpetuate many of the myths and stereotypes ADA was intended to counter.

Because these important issues were not sufficiently addressed by our legislators, employers, employees, and the
courts are left with the difficult job of trying to figure out
what ADA means when it comes to mental disabilities.
Paradoxically, "the Department of Justice and the Equal
Employment Opportunity Commission believe that an accurate understanding of the ADA can prevent the filing of
unnecessary and unfounded charges and support efforts to
resolve disputes arising under the ADA wherever possible
through means other than the filing of charges or lawsuits"
(U.S. EEOC, 1991). However, as already noted, there is nothing in the mental disabilities portion of ADA that is helpful
toward that end. Anyone trying to deal with the problems
this law presents in the realm of the psychological may feel
like Alice in Wonderland. Yandrick (1993) has noted that, as
of July 1993, there remains a dearth of information on how
to accommodate employees with mental disabilities and
about community resources to deal with the problem. One
solution may be forthcoming by the Washington Business
Group on Health, which has recently been funded to create
a data base focused on information relevant to accommodations for mental disabilities.

Despite its flaws, ADA went into effect January 1, 1992,
and all businesses with twenty-five or more employees were
required to be in compliance by July 26. An employer must
provide reasonable accommodation to employees or applicants with mental disabilities if this will help them do
their job and it is not unduly difficult for the employer. ADA
provides for penalties and extensive punitive damages for
violators of the law.

The physical disabilities part of ADA is relatively easy to
understand and came with many guidelines and precedents

to follow. For obvious reasons, determining accommodations for physical disabilities generally follows a logical problem solving approach. This is not the case when it comes to determining accommodations for mental disabilities, an area that remains unclear even for most mental health professionals. Nevertheless, employers should not be discouraged. It is generally agreed that, regardless of the mental disability, it should be neither costly nor difficult to offer reasonable accommodations for most qualified employees. In fact, many businesses already do so.

It has been my fortunate experience to discover that many companies have policies and procedures in place that provide support for employees who have psychological problems. The policies in some businesses also include provisions for the active recruiting and hiring of individuals who are developmentally disabled. However, such policies are far from widespread. Even with the proliferation of programs designed to assist workers with psychological problems, there is research that demonstrates that, in general, workers with mental problems still face highly negative reactions from employers (Farina & Felner, 1973; Combs & Omvig, 1986; Mancuso, 1990). These studies reveal that we have a long way to go before the workplace becomes free of discrimination for people with mental disabilities. ADA holds the business community responsible for making certain this happens and leaves it up to them to comply with the law by developing and implementing formal policies and procedures for accommodating employees with mental disabilities.

This handbook is designed for use by anyone who must confront the difficult issues that will arise in attempting to evaluate requests for accommodations under the mental disabilities part of ADA. In particular, it will be useful to human resource directors, ADA coordinators, corporate counsel, employee assistance personnel, and the EEOC. It is certainly not meant to be the last word, since much is in flux and open to interpretation and controversy when it comes to understanding psychological disorders. It also provides an ADA plan that I believe will protect businesses from charges of noncompliance and unnecessary litigation. Armed with this plan and the other information in this book, businesses can approach ADA with a constructive and healthy attitude that will be of potential benefit to themselves and their employees.

I have written this book from the standpoint of what makes practical sense to a psychologist. My recommendations do not constitute legal advice. Every plan for compliance should be reviewed by legal counsel. Also, until firmer guidelines are established through case law, it is recommended that both legal and psychological consultations be obtained when handling requests for accommodation.

The recommendations in this book are based in part on consultations with other psychologists qualified to comment on the issues raised by ADA. We approached ADA from the point of view of an expert witness as to what is reasonable and makes sense in light of current knowledge regarding mental disorders. I believe that the information provided here will help the business community design and implement plans for handling requests for accommodations and help determine how the law is ultimately interpreted in the courts.

This book promotes the philosophy that every business should take an active, informed stance when developing and implementing a plan to comply with the mental disabilities part of ADA. Companies are encouraged to be prepared to actively evaluate requests for accommodations and not be afraid to challenge diagnoses or requests. I am not, however, encouraging an adversarial stance with regard to ADA; that would not be in keeping with the spirit of the law. I do believe that in addition to avoiding costly litigation, businesses and their employees can profit by seeking successful solutions to the problems presented by employees with psychological problems. This book provides the tools needed to accomplish this task.

1

Myths, Fears, and Stereotypes about Psychological Problems in the Workplace

ADA strives to counter the many myths, fears, and stereotypes about mental disorders so that people will no longer be unfairly discriminated against in the workplace. "Congress acknowledged that society's accumulated myths and fears about disability and diseases are as handicapping as are the physical limitations that flow from an actual impairment" and that common attitudinal barriers have been identified by sociologists "that frequently result in employers excluding individuals with disabilities. These include concerns regarding productivity, safety, insurance liability, attendance, cost of accommodation and accessibility, workers compensation costs, and acceptance by coworkers and customers" (U.S. EEOC & U.S. Department of Justice, 1991).

Many of these beliefs, misperceptions, and attitudes about mental problems and the people who have them are deeply rooted and stem from a lack of knowledge about what it means to have a mental disorder. Even highly educated people possess little or no information about the causes of and treatments for psychological problems and how they may or may not have an impact on work performance.

The following are among the most important myths, fears, and stereotypes about mental disorders as they relate to workplace performance:

1. *A person with psychological problems will perform poorly on the job.* This is a very common myth and one of the reasons why employers have negative attitudes toward people with mental disabilities (Hartlage & Roland, 1971). In fact, a tremendous number of people with psychological impairments nevertheless perform their jobs effectively and efficiently, if not all of the time, then most of the time (Anthony & Jansen, 1984). It has been demonstrated that people who have had psychological problems are indistinguishable from other employees (Howard, 1975). This includes people who may have, by any measure, the most severe mental problems. It is sometimes the case that people with psychological problems perform even better in their jobs because their work gives them an opportunity to distract themselves. Most of these individuals will probably never request or need a workplace accommodation, and employers may never be aware of their personal difficulties. Attendance and safety on the job may also never be an issue, and job performance cannot be predicted on the basis of how someone functions in other areas of their life (Schwartz, Myers, & Astrachan, 1975; Anthony & Farkas, 1982).

During my many years as a clinician I have worked with many troubled people who have had all kinds of jobs. I have seen, among others, designers, physicians, bus drivers, accountants, clerks, company executives, attorneys, and airline pilots. Even though they had significant impairments in one or more areas of their lives, they all had two things in common; they could adequately perform their jobs without accommodations, and they all paid for treatment out of their own pockets. Why? Because they were afraid that if their employers discovered that they had problems they would lose their jobs or, at the very least, be passed over for promotion. ADA was designed to prevent this kind of discrimination.

2. *It is possible to predict how well people can do their jobs from their psychological symptoms.* Numerous studies have demonstrated that there is no relationship between psychological symptoms and future or current ability to work (Ellsworth et al., 1968; Green, Miskimins, & Keil, 1968; Gurel & Lorei, 1972; Lorei, 1967; Schwartz, Myers, & Astrachan, 1975; Strauss & Carpenter, 1972, 1974; Wilson, Berry, & Miskimins, 1969). Moreover, a psychological assessment for psychopathology provides little if any information about an individual's functional work capacity. For example, even though the National Aeronautics and Space Administration (NASA) has spent large sums of money on psychiatric evaluations of astronaut applicants, there is no evidence to demonstrate that these assessments are of any value in predicting on-the-job performance.

There are individuals with what are generally considered the more serious diagnoses of schizophrenia and manic-depression who are perfectly able to do their work. It is sometimes necessary that they be in psychotherapy and take medications. Nevertheless, many can perform the essential functions of their work and may never ask for or need an accommodation. The public unfortunately tends to associate a diagnosis such as schizophrenia with a person's ability to function. However, a diagnosis tells you little of value in and of itself. Far more important is who has the diagnosis and what resources they have to deal with their illness and conduct their lives. Dr. William W. Mayo of the Mayo Clinic once said that it isn't the problem a person has that is important, it is the kind of person who has the problem. Age, general health, previous life experiences, both good and bad, finances, and family support are but a few of the factors that influence the functional abilities and treatment outcome for someone with a psychological impairment. A problem that might severely limit one person's ability to function may not have the same effect for someone else who has family support and the resources to overcome the limitations imposed. One cannot predict an outcome simply on the basis of a diagnosis (Strauss & Carpenter, 1972).

It is therefore not possible to evaluate the functional limitations of individuals to work on the basis of a diagnosis. Moreover, the impairments associated with a diagnosis vary from person to person. It is entirely possible for someone who is diagnosed as phobic or neurotically depressed to be much more impaired than someone with a diagnosis of schizophrenia.

3. *Once a person has been diagnosed as having a mental disorder he or she will always have problems.* Research has revealed that the vast majority of people who have psychological problems at one time or another in their lives eventually go on to lead normal and productive lives. Even people who have had mental problems that resulted in hospitalization may show no evidence of difficulties several years later. In fact, studies have shown that as many as two-thirds of individuals in this category are symptom free on follow-up. What kind of jobs did these people have? There were physicians, lawyers, engineers, teachers, religious leaders, corporate executives, poets, entertainers, artists, musicians, and psychologists. A history of problems is not a reliable predictor of job performance (Cole & Scupe, 1970). However, a history can and has followed individuals for years and been the source of discrimination.

4. *How people function in one setting is predictive of how they will function in other settings.* Research has revealed that how people function in nonvocational activities may have little or nothing to do with their vocational performance. There is a psychological principle that, in most cases, behavior is situation specific, it is difficult to predict how a person will act in different situations. What has been discovered, however, is that the best predictor of a person's future work performance is his or her past employment functioning.

Therefore, if a person has functioned well in previous jobs it is likely that he or she will continue to perform well.

5. *People with mental problems are ill or have a disease.* With the exception of some developmental disorders, there is no conclusive or consistent evidence to support the idea that psychological problems are caused by anything physical. This includes the more serious disorders that have been labeled schizophrenia and manic-depression. There is even some question as to whether there is such a thing as schizophrenia, although there are certainly people who exhibit the sometimes difficult to understand behavior associated with this diagnosis. The World Health Organization avoids the use of the terms "illness" and "disease" in the realm of mental functioning because of the problems associated with them.

The public is generally unaware of the ongoing controversies that surround issues such as diagnoses and causes of mental problems. However, the important thing is that so many people can be helped by psychotherapy and other therapeutic methods even though we do not always know the causes of their problems.

6. *People with psychological problems must take medication.* The majority of people with mental problems do not need to take medication if other options such as psychotherapy are available. Even some people who suffer from the more serious disorders may require medication only temporarily if psychotherapy is available. One of the reasons that so many people take psychiatric medication is that insurance companies have discriminated against individuals with mental problems by restricting treatment options. That is why a Senate bill (SB874-California) was introduced to end this unfair policy. The majority of people with mental disorders can overcome their problems with the help of competent psychotherapists. It is unfortunate that this help has not been available to all Americans in need.

7. *People with mental problems are dangerous or more dangerous than the general population.* There is no evidence that

people with mental disorders are any more dangerous than the general population. The myth that they are more dangerous has unfortunately been perpetuated by movies, other media, and sensationalized cases like that of Charles Manson, among others. People who hurt or kill someone do not have to be insane or crazy, even though some people with psychological problems are indeed dangerous.

8. *People with mental problems are weak or have some kind of personal failing.* It is astonishing that many people still believe this is true. Having psychological problems is no more a personal failing than having a broken leg or a bacterial infection. However, a recent survey by the National Institute of Mental Health discovered that 43 percent of the American public believes that depression is a personal weakness. Two-thirds of those surveyed also said that they would not seek help because of the fear of the stigma and because they did not understand what depression is and how it can be treated. This is infortunate because treatment, especially early on, can be very effective.

9. *It is costly to make accommodations for employees with mental problems.* On the contrary, it is not expensive at all. Most accommodations can be handled with flex-time and by restructuring the work environment. Accommodating employees with mental problems is far less expensive than is the case with physical disabilities.

Once we get beyond the myths, stereotypes, and fears that surround people with psychological problems, we discover that most of these individuals are able to perform their work satisfactorily most of the time. This is all that can really be expected of any employee.

10. *It is possible to predict job performance on the basis of psychological test results.* Research has repeatedly demonstrated that the results of intelligence, aptitude, and personality tests are poor predictors of future job performance (Bidwell, 1969; Goss & Pate, 1967; Sturm & Lipton, 1967). It has been discovered that only those tests that closely simu-

late actual work situations are of value in predicting job performance. All tests and claims should be viewed by employers with skepticism and used with great caution.

It is important to understand these myths, stereotypes, and fears because the incidence of mental disorders in the working population was estimated to be as high as 30 percent in 1970 by the director of the National Institute of Mental Health. That might mean that in a company of 100 employees there could potentially be 30 who are having diagnosable mental problems.

While there is no consensus on exactly how many people may be afflicted with mental disorders, the important fact is that people in the workplace with emotional troubles have been discriminated against irrationally. The ADA was designed to offer these people protection, and it will make it potentially easier for them to work effectively under improved conditions that take into account impairments caused by their mental disorders.

2

Understanding Diagnoses, Impairments, Disabilities, and Handicaps

It is assumed that the majority of employees will request work accommodations on the basis of their having been diagnosed as having a mental disorder. Diagnoses of mental disorders can be made only by qualified mental health professionals using one of the two currently accepted diagnostic classification systems, the American Psychiatric Association's *Diagnostic and Statistical Manual III-Revised* (*DSM III-R*) and the World Health Organization's ICD-10 *Classification of Mental and Behavioural Disorders*. In the United States, the *DSM III-R* (see Appendix 3) is the most frequently used by clinicians, although the *ICD-10* (see Appendix 2) is also used and is approved by insurance companies for reimbursement. The *DSM III-R* is currently undergoing revision; the *DSM-IV* was expected to be completed by 1992 but will not be published until 1994. The *ICD-10* was recently revised, and the new version was published in 1992. Revisions of the two systems have been deliberately timed to appear together, as there is an ongoing effort to make them compatible.

The WHO and APA diagnostic systems are the product of ongoing international efforts by mental health professionals to identify and classify mental and behavioral disorders. Neither is the last word in diagnosis, and it will be many more years, if ever, before a generally agreed upon system finally exists. In the meantime, there will be continuing research and debate over many controversial issues related to attempts at classification and treatment. While this may be confusing to businesses that try to comply with requests for accommodations, they should not be held responsible for errors and misunderstandings that are a result of the controversies among mental health professionals. ADA does not require businesses to become psychologists. However, it is probably prudent to become knowledgeable about some of the basic terminology that will be encountered in dealing with requests. This could make handling requests much easier. The most important of these terms are "diagnosis," "disorder," "impairment," "disability," and "handicap."

A *diagnosis* of a disorder refers to "a clinically recognizable set of symptoms or behaviour associated in most cases with distress and with interference of personal functions" (WHO, 1992). The term "disorder" is preferred by clinicians over terms such as "disease" or "illness" in order to avoid the greater problems inherent in their use. A diagnosis means that a clinician believes that a psychological impairment or impairments exist. For example, the diagnosis of simple phobia is made when an individual fears traveling by air and becomes severely anxious when flying and subsequently avoids it altogether.

"In the context of health experience, an *impairment* is any loss or abnormality of psychological structure or function" (WHO, 1976). For example, in the realm of mental disorders, it may mean that a person has poor interpersonal relationships, or memory or concentration difficulties, insomnia, phobias, emotional control issues, or an eating dysfunction, among other things. According to ADA, any person who has an impairment of a major life activity qualifies as having a disability. However, as I have already noted, there are many people with diagnoses of mental disorders who are not impaired with regard to their ability to work. They may be perceived, however, as having an impairment and still fall under the protection of ADA. For example, a flying phobia would be considered an impairment under ADA if traveling by air is an essential job function. If not, the problem would be covered only if the person was perceived as having a mental disorder and discriminated against because of this perception. In this example, it is unlikely, as the general public tends to view flying phobias as eccentricities rather than mental disorders.

There are many people who have never consulted with a mental health professional but who are, nevertheless, psychologically impaired in some major life activity. These individuals may have adjusted to their impairments in a way that is satisfactory to them, and many accept the status quo. An example of this might be someone with a sexual dysfunction that impinges on their ability to have a satisfactory relationship with a member of the opposite sex. Rather than attempt to correct this with psychotherapy, they may resign themselves to a life of living alone and of restricted socializing. The important issue here is that these people will not be of concern for businesses trying to comply with ADA unless they are perceived as having a mental disorder and discriminated against. Also, employees must identify themselves as having a need for an accommodation before an employer is legally obligated to try to provide one under ADA.

Psychological impairments are generally categorized as either temporary or permanent. The determination of a permanent psychological impairment is much more difficult than that of a physical impairment except in the realm of developmental disorders such as mental retardation. A mental disorder should be rated permanent only after maximum rehabilitation through therapy and other interventions has been exhausted.

In many disability systems such as workers' compensation, psychologically impaired patients are too often rated permanently disabled when even the treating doctors disagree with the medical examiner and maximum rehabilitation has not been achieved. This has had a very destructive effect on many patients (Volle, 1975) and is one of the primary criticisms of disability rating systems. Decisions are often made administratively rather than on the basis of what is happening at a therapeutic level.

The determination of permanency is a complicated and gray area that is made more difficult by the fact that, because of the lengthy treatment required for some people, "temporary" is a relative term and can mean many years. One of the biggest mistakes that can occur in the treatment of mental disorders is to conclude too early or on the basis of a diagnosis or other factors that further improvement is not possible.

One interesting aspect in which ADA differs from disability systems is that there is no designated agency for handling claims or delegating evaluations. The business community is fully responsible for taking on or assigning this function with or without consultation from the EEOC or other legal and professional assistance. Also, the purpose of disability systems such as social security is different and has more to do with establishing financial compensation for the disabled who cannot work than with helping them to work in spite of their disability.

Once employees or prospective employees have identified themselves as having a psychological impairment and request an accommodation, they are considered as having a disability under ADA. "In the context of a health experience, a *disability* is any restriction or lack (resulting from an impairment) of ability to perform an activity in the manner or within the range considered normal for a human being"

(WHO, 1980). In order for a person with a psychological disability to qualify for protection under ADA, he or she must be able to perform the essential function(s) of a job.

ADA holds that "disability" and "handicap" are equivalent terms. However, for practical reasons WHO (1980) has defined a handicap as being different from a disability: "In the context of a health experience, a *handicap* is a disadvantage for a given individual, resulting from an impairment or a disability, that limits or prevents fulfillment of a role that is normal (depending on age, sex, and social and cultural factors) for that individual." For example, not being able to hold a job because of an impairment or disability would be defined as a handicap by WHO. An airline pilot who developed a flying phobia would be considered handicapped.

While qualified mental health professionals provide diagnoses and make evaluations as to the extent and severity of impairments and disabilities, it is the responsibility of employers to make the administrative decisions about actual accommodations. However, it must be remembered that an impairment or impairments and appropriate accommodations cannot be automatically inferred from a diagnosis. For example, two individuals with the same diagnosis may require identical, totally different, or overlapping accommodations. The effect of a mental impairment, that is, the disability it causes, is a separate determination that must be assessed on a case to case basis. Also, it should be remembered that while a mental diagnosis implies a psychological impairment, it does not necessarily mean that an individual is disabled when it comes to work performance. This makes it important for employers to evaluate individual ADA requests carefully and not take any request at face value.

3

Complying with ADA:
A Plan for Mental Disabilities

While ADA was thrust upon the businesses community with minimum guidelines, it is clear that penalties and punitive damages arising out of charges of noncompliance can probably be avoided if a good faith effort has been made to develop and implement a plan to process requests for accommodations. The good news is that this is not difficult or expensive to do.

The Justice Department has said that it will not be going on witch hunts to look for companies that have not complied with ADA. However, if a discrimination claim is filed, the department will likely be very interested to see if a company has made a good faith effort to comply with the law. The following plan was constructed by the staff at the California Institute of Psychology and represents what we believe to be an example of a good faith effort to comply with ADA.

WRITE AND DISTRIBUTE A CLEAR ADA COMPANY POLICY

A company should have a written policy stating that, being in compliance with ADA, it does not discriminate against persons with past, present, or perceived mental problems. It should also state that if someone can perform the essential functions of a job, the company will attempt to make reasonable accommodations for employees or prospective employees who identify themselves as requiring assistance. Make certain that every employee or prospective employee is aware of the policy.

EVALUATE MENTAL HEALTH BENEFITS

If your company provides mental health benefits, it is a good idea to do a thorough evaluation of the quality and type of services available to your employees. The recent trend appears to be in the direction of holding businesses accountable for harm suffered by employees who use mental health workers and plans endorsed by their employer. Also, since some managed care companies routinely discriminate against individuals with certain types of mental disorders, businesses contracting with them could possibly be held liable under ADA. The following quotations convey an idea of problems that occur in some plans.

> We routinely put people on a wait list unless they were in crisis. We never called them back and I don't know if they ever got treatment. It was a big joke among the supervisors.
>> Former therapist for a well known
>> health maintenance organization

> The marketing director told the company that we had Spanish and Chinese speaking therapists and we didn't have any.
>> Assistant director for a managed care company

You will have to over-diagnosis [*sic*] this patient [lie] if
he is going to get the treatment he needs. It will be on
his record but that can't be helped.
        Assessor for a large employee assistance program

These are terrible revelations about some mental health
services. A business that contracts with a managed mental
health care system has every right to expect high quality
services for its employees. However, many health professionals in the front line of delivery encounter an incredible
amount of variation in the quality of these programs. In a
few, there is a genuine commitment to the delivery of first
rate clinical services without unnecessary barriers and
limitations. In others, there is an appalling lack of integrity,
and it appears that every effort is made to discourage both
patients and therapists from engaging in productive therapeutic work. Unfortunately, there seem to be more of the
latter in this industry, which goes virtually unregulated in
many states.

Evaluating managed care is not always an easy task, and
it is sometimes made more difficult by not knowing what
questions should be asked. The following questions will at
least provide enough information to form an opinion of the
integrity of a program. If still in doubt, consult with a
mental health professional who can give you an in-depth
analysis.

1. *What kinds of problems are covered? Is psychotherapy an
option or is crisis intervention the only service?* A managed care
plan should be very clear about the kinds of psychological
problems that will or will not receive treatment. In reality,
most managed care systems allow only for crisis intervention and/or brief treatment. There is nothing wrong with
this if it is explicitly stated; however, some plans are outright
fraudulent and rely on public ignorance about mental health
and treatment.

The worst kind of managed care system is one that leads you to believe that all problems can be handled in twenty sessions or less or claims that certain types of problems or diagnoses are untreatable. Another kind will have you believe that longer-term treatment is available to your employees, but in reality such treatment is discouraged by the review process and harassment of the therapists.

A good plan will have explicit policies and procedures that deal with those individuals whose problems may fall outside the range covered by your program, for example, long-standing personality problems. A good program will also make every effort to direct an employee with an un-covered problem to someone who will be able to provide the necessary treatment.

2. *Who are the providers? Are they personally interviewed or recruited blindly?* In the many years that I have contracted with managed systems, only one company has ever sent someone to interview me. They sent an experienced clinician to do a thorough evaluation of my clinical abilities and credentials, and they would not accept me as a provider unless I had been in practice for five years. Every other company simply checked to see if I had a license, malpractice insurance, and an answering machine. As far as I know, my references have never been reviewed.

Because there is a great deal of variation in the training and experience of therapists, it is extremely important that prospective providers be screened thoroughly for qualifications and experience. However, this is seldom the case. Quality assurance simply cannot exist without good clinicians, regardless of the utilization review procedures in place.

Incidentally, I resigned as a provider from the company that interviewed me because, amazingly, they did not use mental health practitioners for utilization review and pressured me to have my patients inappropriately placed on potentially dangerous medications. I have since discovered that this is not an uncommon practice.

3. *Can an employee self-refer? Do nontherapists or relatively inexperienced therapists screen calls?* The importance of the first contact and subsequent evaluation and accurate diagnosis cannot be overestimated when it comes to mental conditions. However, this is another weak point in the majority of managed mental health care programs. Evaluations are often left to those least qualified to make competent clinical assessment, and this is a recognized problem in the industry. The best programs allow employees to self-refer to highly qualified professionals without having to go through a maze of paperwork or multiple evaluations prior to receiving services. While it may not seem important, seeing one person for an evaluation and another for treatment often has negative consequences. There is no clinical justification for setting up a system in this manner.

4. *How is quality assurance maintained?* The best quality assurance is to contract with highly trained and experienced psychotherapsits who can evaluate and treat a problem at the lowest cost in the shortest time possible. A marketing strategy used by a few managed care companies is to imply that there are unscrupulous psychotherapists who prolong therapy unnecessarily and make it more costly. While this is undoubtedly true in a few cases, a good screening of potential providers would, for the most part, eliminate this problem. When good therapists are used, quality assurance does not require supervision and unnecessary reviews with tons of paperwork. The procedures may look impressive, but they add little to the business at hand, that is, helping people recover from psychological problems.

Recent research has demonstrated that the utilization review process does not have an impact on cost containment or the quality of care. There are many very good therapists who have refused to become providers for managed care systems because of excessive paperwork and difficulties dealing with the reviewers, who frequently are not licensed therapists.

5. *Does your company receive regular utilization reports and cost-effectiveness estimates?* A company deserves to have regularly supplied information on numbers of referrals and outcome. This can easily be accomplished without breaking confidentiality. A managed care company should also provide regular reports that demonstrate cost-effectiveness.

6. *Are there procedures to assure confidentiality of employees using mental health services?* Effective psychotherapy can only take place when there is an assurance of confidentiality. To this end, there are laws that guarantee this privilege except under certain circumstances. A good managed care system should have a procedure in place so that an employee's identity is totally disguised and inaccessible to anyone else. Names, social security numbers, and other identifying information should not appear on insurance or other forms that can be accessed by anyone who does not have a legitimate reason to deal with the paperwork. It is a simple matter to set up a code system managed by a psychotherapist; this would give the maximum guarantee that confidentiality is maintained.

Summary

As of this writing, managed mental health care is an unregulated industry without ethical guidelines for the mental health workers who participate as providers or in other capacities. While there are proposals to make these companies accountable for their clinical actions and decisions, the evidence is that many continue to use fraudulent claims to sell services that are potentially dangerous to the health of enrollees. Every business should take the time to become informed about provision of mental health treatment and what constitutes quality care.

EVALUATE EMPLOYEE ASSISTANCE PROGRAMS

A few years ago it was discovered that, following the suicide of an employee in New York, the employee assistance program (EAP) director, who prescribed treatment and was actively counseling the employee, had only a master's degree in psychology. Up until a month earlier she had been the employment manager of the company and was not a licensed mental health practitioner. As this case demonstrates, a business must be confident that the staff chosen to evaluate, diagnose, refer, and/or treat employees are professionally qualified to do so.

Employee assistance programs have become increasingly popular since the 1950s, when they were first introduced to deal with employee alcohol problems. The popularity of EAPs has been due in part to studies that revealed cost benefits to companies that got treatment for their problem employees rather than firing them. These cost benefits accrued because of increases in employee productivity and reduction of the costs of hiring and training replacements. In the early days EAPs were staffed with individuals familiar with alcohol related problems; many of them had been through treatment programs themselves. However, over the years EAPs have offered more and more services and have become known as broad-brush programs because they deal with all kinds of employee problems. Moreover, while the range of problem areas dealt with by EAPs has increased, the expertise of staff has not always kept pace.

In the April 1990 issue of *Employee Assistance*, Dr. Paul M. Roman wrote regarding the status of EAPs, "I despair at the minimal attention given to referral . . . referral effectiveness is given practically no attention, yet I would argue it may be the most important single factor in long-term employee assistance cost-effectiveness." He also addressed the issue of accountability for referrals to proper treatment. This is the most serious issue because many EAPs have unqualified staff who inaccurately diagnose, improperly treat, or fail to treat employees. This was highlighted by Dr. Bradley K. Googins in the same issue of the periodical: "The person sitting in the EAP chair has to be prepared to explore the nature of the presenting problem, not simply to take on face value the symptoms brought up on first contact and prescribe treatment." Yet, as he goes on to point out, "the role of [diagnosis] is generally not mentioned, nor discussed at any great length in EAP literature." This is truly remarkable, as the identification (diagnosis) of a problem is the first critical step in determining an appropriate treatment. According to an American Psychological Association task force, this lack of expertise in managed health care will lead to lawsuits against EAP staff and companies as employees become more knowledgeable about what constitutes acceptable levels of care. A close look at several EAPs reveals that this problem exists even when, judging from outward appearances such as licenses and degrees, the staff seem to be highly qualified.

An interview with a former intern and assistant director of EAP clinical services at one of the largest banks in the United States revealed considerable problems. For example, on the quality of the EAP staff: "The [EAP] counselors are so bad clinically that they simply don't know to refer to a good therapist because they don't know how to evaluate a therapist any better than they can accurately evaluate employee problems. Also, because of their lack of training they don't know when it is appropriate to refer for specific types of treatment." On quality assurance and effectiveness of treatment: "There was no policy on follow-up studies. We had no idea if an employee went for treatment more than once. We also didn't know if they got any help." In this EAP, the majority of staff are trainees, and most if not all do not have the type of training necessary for good clinical work even though they have advanced degrees in clinical psychology. Because they lack proper training, they are simply not equipped to detect more subtle problems and refer for appropriate treatment.

These two basic problem areas, qualifications of EAP staff and lack of outcome information upon which to evaluate an EAP, are of serious concern. The same issues also exist in many if not most external EAP programs. These EAPs promise high quality assurance to companies, but in fact have no process to determine either the clinical capabilities of the therapists with whom they contract or to evaluate the outcome of treatments. If someone has a valid license and malpractice insurance, and agrees to work within their "treatment" model, they can become a provider. Also, many of these companies operate with a hotline, usually covered by a counselor or nonprofessional who screens calls from employees and then makes referrals. These EAPs are very explicit about letting therapists know that they expect as many cases as possible to be taken care of quickly. "It is expected that the majority of Clients will have their needs for consultation satisfied within 1-5 sessions," reads the contract of a major international supplier of EAPs. A California based managed health plan states, "We stress a brief psychotherapy model for treatment . . . a time limited approach is tried first." Even though the medical director of this company says that they will refer for the most appropriate treatment, an EAP counselor of a company that uses this system stated that she had never seen an employee's benefits extended when a more in-depth treatment was indicated.

If your business uses an EAP, the following questions will help begin the process of evaluating its integrity:

1. *What are the clinical qualifications of the person in charge of our EAP?* This person should be highly trained in the assessment and treatment of a wide range of emotional problems. He/she should be able to detect underlying problems and refer for the most effective treatment possible. This position carries with it the utmost responsibility for employees and the integrity of the EAP. This individual should be able not only to provide clinical services but also to supervise other EAP staff when necessary. The training background of the most qualified clinician will include at least several years of both inpatient and outpatient experience in a major medical setting. This would include training in both short- and long-term treatment approaches with the widest range of psychological problems. Having a license is not a guarantee that your EAP provider is necessarily qualified.

2. *What kind of information management system is in place to provide both quantitative and qualitative information about the use and effectiveness of the EAP?* There should be regularly documented outcome data based on a systematic solicitation of feedback from employees that use the EAP. This feedback should consist of information about employee satisfaction and dissatisfaction with the process and treatment. There should be a systematic, ongoing cost-benefit analysis that reflects the EAP's utility to the company in dollar terms. All of this information should be readily available to management on a regular basis. The issue is clear. If a company chooses to have an EAP or any other type of managed mental health benefit, it must be prepared to evaluate that program to insure the safety of its employees. It is not enough to depend upon the claims of the managed mental health care providers. You must be well enough informed to judge for yourself.

EAPs have been described as the ideal organization for implementing ADA plans if they are staffed with qualified mental health professionals. There are, however, potential conflicts of interest for clinicians who work in this area that must be attended to. For example, the first ethical loyalty of all mental health professionals is to their patients. In the case of clinicians who work for businesses, they are sometimes placed in a dual role that may compromise their professional integrity. These issues should be directly addressed by all of the personnel involved in implementing an ADA plan as well as in processing requests.

CREATE JOB DESCRIPTIONS THAT INCLUDE THE MENTAL FUNCTIONS NECESSARY TO DO A JOB

ADA says that businesses do not have to evaluate the essential functions of a job prior to a request for an accommodation. It has been pointed out, however, that it may be prudent to have written job descriptions to avoid undue complications if charged with violations of ADA. Companies should update current descriptions and delineate the mental functions necessary to do jobs. Most companies that already have descriptions of the behavioral and physical requirements for workers do not have similar descriptions for psychological functions.

It is a good idea for businesses to at least familiarize themselves with a list of psychological job descriptors for future reference. I have constructed a checklist of mental functions (Appendix 4) that will be helpful toward this end. It should be noted that these descriptors represent those most commonly used in the psychological literature; the list is not meant to be exhaustive or the final word of what is acceptable.

An example of psychological job descriptors for a particular position might be as follows: Bartender—cheerful and pleasant toward customers; good judgment in handling problems with customers; good attention and ability to shift to new tasks; memory capacity large enough to handle six to eight orders at once; able to write and follow directions; can perform basic arithmetic.

EDUCATE EMPLOYEES ABOUT THE CAUSES AND TREATMENT OF PSYCHOLOGICAL PROBLEMS

The majority of people in the United States, including the well educated, have little or no knowledge of the causes and treatments of mental disorders. This is extremely unfortunate because this lack of knowledge prevents many people from getting the help they need early on and prolongs their suffering.

It has been demonstrated repeatedly that it is cost-effective for businesses to help their employees become informed consumers of medical and psychological services. Educated employees seek out proper help early, and this results in reduced absenteeism and time off because of illnesses. Therefore, in addition to demonstrating a good faith effort to comply with ADA, employee education is also financially rewarding for businesses.

It is neither expensive nor time consuming to offer workshops, seminars, and written materials about the causes and treatment of mental disorders.

HAVE CLEAR WRITTEN PROCEDURES FOR HOW EMPLOYEE REQUESTS FOR ACCOMMODATIONS ARE PROCESSED AND WHO EMPLOYEES SHOULD CONTACT

To smooth the way for employees to identify themselves as requiring an accommodation, it is important to make the process well known to employees and as confidential as possible. This means having clearly defined procedures and designated personnel to handle requests.

The officially designated individual(s) or department could be an administrative person such as a human resources director or a mental health professional in a company employee assistance program. It is generally agreed that employee assistance program personnel may be the most suitable for handling requests, as they are mental health professionals and also understand the workings of a business. In companies without an EAP, it would be feasible to designate either the director of human resources or an outside consultant as the mental disabilities coordinator.

DOCUMENT EVERYTHING YOU HAVE DONE TO EDUCATE YOURSELF AND YOUR EMPLOYEES ABOUT THE MENTAL DISABILITIES PART OF ADA

This recommendation almost goes without saying since it has become a routine aspect of how businesses legally protect themselves. Include readings, seminars, and consultations with mental health workers and labor law attorneys. This information may be of importance in demonstrating that a good faith effort has been made to comply with ADA if a company is charged with being in violation of the law. It is generally agreed that businesses will be able to avoid punitive damages if they make such an effort.

4

Qualified Mental Health Professionals and Employee Assistance Programs

While not explicitly stated in ADA, the determination of diagnoses, impairments, disabilities, and handicaps should be the judgment of professionals who are qualified and licensed to assess mental functioning in accordance with generally accepted standards. These include mental health professionals (MHPs) such as psychologists (Ph.D., Ed.D., Psy.D.), psychiatrists (M.D.), social workers (L.C.S.W. or M.S.W.), and marriage, family, and child counselors (M.F.C.C.). Different states use different titles for people who are licensed and have a master's degree, such as M.F.C.C. It is not advisable for company personnel other than qualified EAP staff to attempt to evaluate the mental status of an employee.

While MHPs have different levels of training and expertise, ADA has not established a particular set of guidelines or requirements for those MHPs who will be involved in ADA related functions. Essentially, any MHP who is licensed to diagnose and treat patients with mental disorders will probably, at least in the beginning, be acceptable as a qualified examiner. However, this may change when the EEOC gains some experience with ADA cases.

However, whether a business is relying on the professionals in an employee assistance program or MHPs from the community, it is entitled to know whether or not they are licensed by the state as well as how much training they have had and where it was received.

A minimum requirement for all MHPs is that they possess the license or certificate required to practice their profession. However, businesses should be aware that degrees and licenses do not necessarily mean competence to diagnose and treat the full range of mental disorders, and therefore all requests for accommodation should not be taken at face value, for the protection of both the employer and the employee. Each request should be carefully evaluated for its legitimacy and validity. Businesses should either use qualified MHPs in their own EAP or have consultants who are well trained and experienced and who understand ADA and other workplace issues.

Businesses will encounter several kinds of mental health professionals in handling ADA requests for accommodation:

PSYCHOLOGIST (PH.D., PSY.D., OR ED.D.)

Psychologists have a doctorate in psychology and receive extensive training in psychological testing and psychotherapy. They are licensed in every state to diagnose and treat people with psychological disorders. In many states, such as California, this also includes patients with disorders serious enough to require hospitalization.

Many psychologists, but not all, are graduates of formal training programs called internships. Others may develop their clinical skills in privately arranged supervision and seminars. These professionals are not currently licensed to prescribe medications, although this may become part of their training in the near future. However, most psychologists receive education and training about when medications are indicated and will consult with a psychiatrist to obtain medication for their patients.

PSYCHIATRIST (M.D.)

All psychiatrists are physicians, but not all psychiatrists are graduates of formal training programs called residencies. A physician can call himself or herself a psychiatrist without specialized training, although it is foolish to do so. Those doctors who have completed a training program in psychiatry (residency) can call themselves "board eligible." Those who have passed the examination of their professional organization are "board certified."

All psychiatrists who have completed residencies receive training in the prescription of drugs for mental disorders. However, some may receive little or no training in how to do psychotherapy. In other words, not all psychiatrists are psychotherapists.

SOCIAL WORKER (L.C.S.W., M.S.W.)

Social workers often obtain training in the diagnosis and treatment of mental disorders. Many, but not all, have received their clinical experience in formal training programs. However, some may have received excellent training through privately arranged supervision and seminars.

MARRIAGE, FAMILY, AND CHILD COUNSELOR (M.F.C.C.)

The M.F.C.C. degree is relatively new. Some of the practitioners who have completed this course of training receive high quality education and clinical training.

There are individuals from all four of the above groups who may also specialize in the practice of psychoanalysis, which requires further education and training.

Employee assistance programs (EAPs) have been described as the ideal department for helping companies implement ADA and process requests for accommodations. However, all EAPs are not the same, and some do not have the expertise necessary to diagnose or treat the full range of mental disorders. As suggested in the previous chapter, companies with EAPs should carefully evaluate their programs to be certain they are staffed with professionals who are suitable to evaluate ADA requests. Also, even if a company does have an EAP perfectly suited to serve the purposes of ADA, certain problems may arise that will require special attention.

For example, there is the potential that an EAP could be accused of conflict of interest by a disgruntled employee. It is obvious that mental health workers who staff the EAP offices of companies are serving two masters, and their roles are not always clearly defined even though they are ethically bound to put patients' interests first.

The primary obligation of every psychotherapist is to the individuals who come to him or her for help. A therapist who works for a business and who sees employees for evaluations or therapy must always be on guard that company loyalties do not interfere with his or her ethical obligations. With regard to ADA, it is important that EAP staff be sensitive to conflicts of interest; they should use an outside consultant when in doubt, and if an agreeable accommodation with an employee cannot be reached.

5

Treatment of Psychological Disorders

Employers may find themselves confused about the different treatment approaches used by mental health professionals. In some cases, it will seem odd that employees with the same diagnosis are being treated with different therapies. Much of the confusion may be alleviated, however, if it is remembered that a diagnosis does not necessarily indicate what treatment might be best for any given individual.

The prescription of therapy for any particular individual is, or should be, a decision based on the evaluation of a number of factors, of which the diagnosis is only one. For example, for one person with the diagnosis of schizophrenia, psychoanalysis may be the most appropriate treatment. For another, drug treatment with supportive psychotherapy might be the treatment of choice. Because of prevailing attitudes toward people with emotional problems and an ignorance of how and when psychotherapy can help, many people have been denied appropriate treatment. Moreover, it has not been in the best interests of the public that the largely unregulated managed care industry has gained control of the gates to therapy and denied so many people the treatment they need. With this in mind, it is even more important for employers to take the time to gain knowledge of psychotherapy.

Psychotherapy is a group of methods that psychotherapists use to help people get over their problems. Psychotherapists must study and train for many years before they become skilled in using these methods. Most therapists specialize in treating certain kinds of problems with specific kinds of therapy.

The kind of therapy a psychotherapist uses should be determined by the kind of problem a person has, his or her personal resources, and other factors such as convenience and ability to pay.

There is not any one psychotherapy that works for everyone. It depends on who the person is and the type of problem. Also, financial or geographical reasons may limit the therapists and therapies that are available.

Therapy may take only a short time in some cases, while in others it may take several years. Accidents, traumatic events, or a change in life circumstances may set off a hidden problem which will require some time in treatment. Moreover, it is not possible in the beginning to tell exactly how long therapy will take. If problems have existed for a long time and affect many parts of a person's life, it can be expected that therapy will last for a year or more.

In some therapies, a therapist is seen only once a week. In others it may be necessary to visit several times a week. Seeing a therapist more than once a week does not necessarily mean that a problem is worse. It may simply mean that a particular therapy works best with more frequent visits.

Individual therapy sessions generally last forty-five to fifty minutes. Group therapy sessions are sometimes ninety minutes to two hours.

TYPES OF PSYCHOTHERAPY

It is not possible to discuss all of the different types of therapy. Many people have read or heard about cognitive therapy, behavior therapy, psychoanalysis, and psycho-analytic psychotherapy as well as brief, short-term, or long-term therapy. However, whatever the therapy, it should be the best one for a person, given their problem and situation. Therefore, a therapist should have the training and ex-perience to allow him or her to make a proper evaluation and determine what is the best treatment.

The following is a general way of categorizing therapies:

The Talking Therapies

These methods can be either brief, short-term, or long-term depending on the kind of problem and the person who has the problem, among other things. Sometimes a problem requires only a few sessions; other problems may require hundreds of sessions.

Individual Therapy

These therapies focus on the individual and his or her problems in a one-to-one relationship with a psycho-therapist. Depending on the problem and the patient, the therapist will either make suggestions about what to do or will help patients to learn about themselves in a way that will help them deal better with their conflicts.

In many cases people are not aware of all the reasons why they are having a particular problem or problems. As an outside observer, a therapist can help them become aware of the reasons so that they can find new solutions.

Group Therapy

Group therapy can be used alone or along with individual therapy. Groups are often formed for people with specific problems such as phobias, alcohol abuse, or relationship difficulties. This can be a very effective kind of therapy for some people. Groups usually have six to eight members and either one or two therapists.

Marital and Couples Therapy

Marital and couples therapy can help salvage relationships that are falling apart or help partners end a relationship with the least amount of damage. Sometimes it helps if the partners go to a group for couples.

Family Therapy

This approach can be helpful when one or more family members have a problem that is affecting everyone else. Arrangements are made for all or most family members to meet weekly with a therapist or sometimes two therapists. The therapist works with all the family members in order to change both individual and family behavior so that the family can coexist in harmony.

Child and Adolescent Therapy

When children and teenagers have problems at home, in school, or with peers, a psychotherapist can often be very helpful. Young patients can be seen in individual therapy, in groups, or with the whole family.

Therapy with children and adolescents may include playing board games, in a sandbox, or with toys, as well as talking. It depends on what the therapist thinks will work best for the child.

Drug Therapy

Drugs do not cure psychological problems. Except for certain exceptions, they are not a replacement for psychotherapy, and they won't make psychological problems go away. Unfortunately, psychiatric drugs are used far too often and can have a destructive impact on the potential for getting better.

However, medications can be of great value in cases when they make it possible for a person to work on his or her problems in therapy. Drugs should only be used when a person is having difficulty functioning to a serious degree.

As with all drugs, side effects are possible when taking psychiatric medications; these can be both psychological and physical. It is the right of patients to fully understand the possible side effects of any drugs.

While it may be comforting to believe that the causes of psychological problems are biological, everyone should be aware that there is no scientific proof that this is true.

Electroconvulsive Treatment (ECT)

ECT is reserved for severe depressions and other problems when a person has become almost totally dysfunctional. While there are many fears and misunderstandings about ECT, it is painless and without danger in the hands of competent doctors. It is usually the last choice when other treatments have failed. It can cause dramatic improvement in many cases. This treatment is used for only the most serious of cases and is done only in a hospital.

Pop Therapies

There is no end to the number of "junk food" therapies, which come and go as quickly as the people who invent them. Remember how popular Erhard seminar training (EST) was a few years ago. While these so-called therapies hold out great hope for people with problems, they are generally a waste of time and money, although they may make some people feel better for a time.

Whether we like it or not, it is usually very difficult for human beings to change unwanted behavior and feelings.

Everyone should be wary of offers for simple or short-term solutions to problems, especially problems that have been around for a long time. Human beings are very complicated, and it sometimes takes a great deal of hard work and time to change.

Behavior Therapy

Behavior therapy is a set of methods designed to change very specific behaviors, such as smoking, drinking alcohol, or overeating. It also may help reduce fears of specific things or places.

In this therapy, the patient and therapist focus on those situations that lead to the unwanted behavior. A goal is set and a step by step plan is laid out and followed. As one goal is achieved, others may be added.

Cognitive-Behavior Therapy

Cognitive-behavior therapy is based on the idea that a person can change unwanted behavior by learning to think and feel in new ways.

In this therapy, the patient is usually expected to practice homework assignments. For example, he or she might be asked to imagine acting in a new way in a situation that is upsetting.

Reality Therapy

Reality therapy is a treatment that focuses on behavior rather than feelings. A therapist will help patients to look at what they do to avoid reality and/or stay away from certain uncomfortable parts of daily life. Through learning what aspects of life are being avoided, a therapist may be able to help patients behave in more positive ways.

Psychoanalysis

This method is often called an insight oriented or uncovering approach. The goal in this form of treatment is to help a person become aware of the reasons for his or her problems. It is through this process that change may occur.

The average length of treatment is about five years, with four or five sessions a week. The patient usually lies on a couch and free associates, that is, says whatever comes to mind. The therapist/analyst listens very carefully and helps the patient understand his or her thoughts and feelings.

Psychoanalytic Psychotherapy

Psychoanalytic psychotherapy is similar to psychoanalysis. However, the main differences are that in psychoanalytic psychotherapy the patient may be seen one to three times a week and may sit facing the therapist.

Hypnosis

Hypnosis is usually a brief form of therapy aimed at taking care of specific problems quickly. It is sometimes used along with other psychotherapies. In hypnosis, a patient is put into a trance and information is obtained which the therapist uses in the attempt to resolve the patient's problems.

Humanistic and Existential Therapies

This group of approaches to therapy focuses on the ability of people to grow and learn. By looking at "here and now" experiences and feelings a person may become more aware and have more choices. These types of therapies place less importance on early life experiences.

Transactional Analysis (TA)

TA is a form of therapy that teaches patients that they have three basic ways of reacting to each other: as "parent," "adult," and "child." Everyone is seen as having a particular "drama" or "script" that they live out and "games" that they play. By pointing out patients' games and scripts, the therapist may help them change.

Eclectic Therapy

"Eclectic" means that a therapist uses a number of methods drawn from different types of therapy, such as those listed above. Actually, most therapists work this way, though many have one method they usually rely on.

SUMMARY

As I mentioned at the beginning of this chapter, employers may be confused by the different treatment methods employed by mental health professionals. To clear up some of the confusion, remember that the same diagnoses may require different treatment approaches in different individuals. This will in turn mean that different accommodations may be necessary for these employees in terms of the time demands of treatment.

6

Common Mental Disorders and Sample Accommodations

The majority of accommodations for employees with mental disorders are either inexpensive or free and can be handled quite easily through time off for therapy, flexible work schedules, restructuring the work environment, and/or eliminating auxiliary job functions. Mancuso (1990) has provided a list of options that should be considered when attempting to work out a reasonable accommodation for an employee with a mental disability. Among these are:

A. Changes in Interpersonal Communication:
   1. Arranging for all work requests to be put in writing for a library assistant who becomes anxious and confused when given verbal instructions;
   2. Training a supervisor to provide positive feedback along with criticisms of performance for an employee reentering the work force who needs reassurance of his/her abilities after a long psychiatric hospitalization;

3. Allowing a worker who personalizes negative comments about his/her work performance to provide a self-appraisal before receiving feedback from a supervisor;

4. Scheduling planning sessions with a co-worker at the start of each day to develop hourly goals for someone who functions best with added time structure.

B. Modifications to the Physical Environment:

1. Purchasing room dividers for a data entry operator who has difficulty maintaining concentration (and thus accuracy) in an open work area;

2. Arranging for an entry-level worker to have an enclosed office to reduce noise and interruptions that provoke disabling anxiety.

C. Job Modification:

1. Arranging for someone who cannot drive or use public transportation to work at home;

2. Restructuring a receptionist job by eliminating lunchtime switchboard duty normally handled by someone in this position;

3. Exchanging problematic secondary tasks for part of another employee's job description.

D. Schedule Modification:

1. Allowing a worker with poor physical stamina to extend his/her schedule to allow for additional breaks or rest periods during the day;

2. Allowing a worker to shift his/her schedule (as necessary) to attend psychotherapy appointments.

Chafkin (1993) of the President's Committee on Employment of People with Disabilities has provided a different grouping of options, as follows:

I. Flexibility
   a. Providing leave for mental health problems.
   b. Providing self-paced workload and flexible hours.
   c. Allowing people to work at home, providing needed equipment.
   d. Providing more job-sharing opportunities.
   e. Keeping the job open and providing a liberal leave policy (e.g., granting up to two months of unpaid leave, if it does not cause undue hardship on the employer).
   f. Providing back-up coverage when the employee needs a special or extended leave.
   g. Providing the ability to move laterally, change jobs, or change supervisors within the same organization so that the person can find a good job.
   h. Providing time off for professional counseling.
   i. Providing flexible leave for mental health problems.
   j. Allowing exchange of work duties.
   k. Providing conflict resolution mechanisms.

II. Supervision
   a. Providing written job descriptions.
   b. Providing significant levels of structure, one-to-one supervision, dealing with both content and interpersonal skills.
   c. Providing easy access to supervisor.
   d. Providing guidelines for feedback on problem areas, and developing strategies to anticipate and deal with problems before they arise.
   e. Arranging for an individual to work under a supportive and understanding supervisor.
   f. Providing individualized agreements.

III. Emotional Supports
   a. Providing ongoing, on-the-job peer counseling.

b. Providing praise and positive reinforcement.

c. Being tolerant of a different behavior.

d. Making counseling/employee assistance programs (including stress, disability, family issues,
etc.) available for all employees.

e. Allowing telephone calls during work hours to
friends or others for needed support.

f. Providing substance abuse recovery support
groups and one-to-one counseling.

g. Providing support for people in the hospital (e.g.,
visits, cards, telephone calls).

h. Providing an advocate to advise and support the
employee.

IV. Physical Accommodations at the Workplace

a. Modifying work area to minimize distractions.

b. Modifying work area for privacy.

c. Providing an environment which is smokefree
and well ventilated, has reduced noise, natural
light, easy access to the outside, etc.

d. Providing accommodation for any additional
impairment (e.g., if an employee with a psychiatric impairment also has a visual or mobility
impairment, he/she may need accommodations such as large print for written materials, a
three-wheeled scooter, speech synthesizers for
computers, etc.).

V. Wages and Benefits

a. Providing adequate wages and benefits.

b. Providing health insurance coverage that does
not exclude preexisting conditions, including
psychiatric disabilities, human immunodeficiency virus (HIV), cancer, etc.

c. Permitting sick leave for emotional well-being,
in addition to physical well-being.

    d. Providing assistance with child care, transportation, etc.

    e. Providing specialized training opportunities.

VI. Dealing with Co-workers' Attitudes

    a. Providing sensitivity training for co-workers.

    b. Facilitating open discussions with workers, both with and without disabilities, to articulate feelings and develop strategies to deal with these issues.

    c. Developing a system of rewards and penalties for co-workers without disabilities, based on their acceptance and support for their co-workers with a disability.

The determination of a reasonable accommodation can also be facilitated by adding psychological descriptors to job descriptions. A list of these is provided in Appendix 4. Each request, however, must be evaluated on its own merits, and it is unreasonable to expect that there ever will be a guide that provides simple equations between mental disabilities and specific accommodations. Experience with the Rehabilitation Act of 1973 (RA) may be useful in terms of understanding how ADA may evolve.

Statistics reveal that from 1985 to 1990, 564 mental disability complaints filed under RA were closed. Of the complaints, 52 percent involved psychiatric impairments and 37 percent were related to substance abuse. A minority of cases (11 percent) involved head injuries or mental retardation (Moss, 1992). These data give us some idea of what to expect in terms of the frequency and types of claims that may occur under ADA, although the difficulty in implementing RA may lead the EEOC to pursue more effective means to enforce ADA, and this may increase complaints.

The official agency for handling complaints under RA is the Office of Federal Contract Compliance Programs (OFCCP). This office assigns each mental disability complaint to a category with a three-digit disability code. These categories are meant to be descriptive of certain classes of mental disorders but do not, for the most part, reflect current nomenclature or usage by mental health professionals relying on either the *DSM-III-R* or the *ICD-10*. The OFCCP currently uses the following categories of mental disorders (Moss, 1992):

Neuropsychiatric

- 150 Psychoneurosis, including anxiety state, "compensation neurosis"
- 151 Personality disorder
- 153 Post-psychotic, after recovery from schizophrenia mania-depressive, involutional reaction
- 154 Head injuries, residual effects
- 155 Alcoholism
- 156 Drug addiction

Retardation

- 160 Mentally retarded

While some of these terms are still in current usage, "neuropsychiatry," "psychoneurosis," "mania-depressive," and "involutional reaction" are outdated and seldom if ever used in clinical practice or found in contemporary scientific literature. Also, the categories do not reflect the full range of categories of mental disorders currently in use by mental health professionals. It is not known what impact the limitation of the OFCCP's list has had on complaints or investigations, but it does reflect a lack of congruency with actual clinical usage that should be remedied by the EEOC to reflect contemporary reality.

The following are many of the diagnoses that businesses can expect to encounter when handling ADA requests for accommodation. I have not included every diagnosis listed in the *ICD-10* because some (e.g., multiple personality disorder) are very rare and/or controversial and will probably not be seen very often in requests for accommodation.

It must be emphasized that diagnoses do not convey a total picture of a person's capacities or abilities. People diagnosed as mentally retarded generally show much variation in terms of their potential to respond to educational efforts and the ultimate functional level they achieve. That is why it is so important to evaluate each individual on a case to case basis in order to determine the type and extent of impairment and disability involved.

The following are among the more commonly diagnosed mental disorders that may be encountered in requests for accommodations. The diagnoses, associated impairments, and disabilities are based primarily on *The ICD-10 Classification of Mental and Behavioural Disorders* (1992) and the *International Classification of Impairments, Disabilities, and Handicaps* (1989) because these systems are the most comprehensive and integrated, and therefore helpful, in terms of technical needs under ADA. The suggested accommodations are mine and are not meant to be the last word. For some individuals a certain amount of creativity might be required to arrive at an accommodation, and for others there may be no reasonable accommodation to be found.

It should also be emphasized that, in many cases, the need for an accommodation may be temporary because improvement can generally be expected if an employee is in psychotherapy. For definitions of particular terms such as thinking or family role disability, see appendices 1 and 2.

NEUROTIC, STRESS-RELATED, AND SOMATOFORM DISORDERS F40-F48

The primary symptoms of these orders are anxiety and avoidant behavior. In some disorders anxiety may be the predominant symptom, and in others avoidance may take precedence.

Phobic Anxiety Disorders F40

Agoraphobia F40.00

Agoraphobia generally refers to fear and avoidance of open spaces. It may be designated with or without panic disorder. As with all phobias, a person with this condition may not demonstrate any significant psychological impairment as long as what is feared can be avoided. However, in the presence of open places, an individual with agoraphobia will experience an intense fear and desire to escape accompanied by physical and psychological symptoms. The former may include loss of bladder or bowel control. The latter may and usually do include temporary and general impairment of most psychological functions.

Impairment

a. Impairment of memory.

b. Impairment of thinking.

c. Impairment of consciousness.

d. Impairment of behavior pattern.

e. Impairment of perception and attention.

f. Impairment of volition.

Disability

a. Situation coping disability.

b. Other family role disability.

c. Occupational role disability.

d. Other behavioral disability.

Accommodation

Schedule modification: The most obvious accommodation for agoraphobia is to allow work at home if this is a reasonable option. In a few cases where independent travel is too anxiety provoking, it is conceivable that a person could be driven to and from work by a friend or family member.

Phobias F40.1

The defining characteristic of this disorder is the avoidance of situations (for example, crowds) that evoke extreme anxiety. As in specific (isolated) phobias, the anxiety is often accompanied by secondary symptoms such as fear of losing control or dying. Theoretically, there can be as many different phobias as there are situations. However, the list of actual social phobias reported is limited to a small number of rather common types such as crowds and certain public activities.

Impairment

The important consideration in this disorder is anxiety that, in the presence of the phobic object or situation, may increase to panic proportions. As in agoraphobia, an individual may be temporarily impaired in most psychological functions during an episode. If a person is able to successfully avoid what is feared, she or he may never appear to have an impairment.

a. Impairment of memory.

b. Impairment of thinking.

c. Impairment of perception and attention.

d. Impairment of volition.

Disability

The impairments associated with a social phobia disorder may cause disabilities that range in severity depending on other factors. For example, an employee with a phobia toward public speaking may not exhibit a disability if her or his job functions do not require this activity. Disabilities associated with social phobias may include:

a. Situation coping disability.

b. Occupational role disability.

c. Social role disability.

Accommodation

Workplace accommodations for individuals with phobias can be fairly obvious and simple and may usually involve job modifications. For example, an employee with a phobia of heights could be moved to a lower floor or away from windows. A person with a flying phobia could be allowed to use ground transportation, as is the case with a national sports announcer who drives to his assignments.

While it may be relatively simple to make reasonable accommodations for many employees with this condition, it makes good business sense to support psychotherapy to overcome it. For example, flying phobias can often be eliminated by one session of specialized treatment.

Other Anxiety Disorders F41

Panic Disorder F41.0

This disorder is characterized by panic (severe and escalating anxiety) that cannot be attributed to any external situation or object. The panic is accompanied by, among other things, rapid heartbeat, dizziness, fleeing or desire to flee, and feelings that things are not real. This can be an extremely demoralizing disorder, and people who experience the attacks may be further incapacitated by the fear of recurrence. Attacks may occur with varying frequency.

Impairment

An individual experiencing a panic attack is completely overwhelmed psychologically. Generally, the attacks pass quickly, but they can occur at any time without warning. The condition is often made worse when a person becomes anxious and fearful on a more or less continuous basis, and this can cause further impairments:

a. Impairment of thinking.

b. Impairment of consciousness.

c. Impairment of perception and attention.

d. Impairment of volition.

e. Impairment of behavior pattern.

Disability

A person who has panic attacks may also become avoidant and agoraphobic, that is, afraid of being away from the safety of home. Agoraphobia is frequently diagnosed with or without panic disorder. The diagnosis may be difficult and depends on what came first and the intensity of the symptoms.

A panic disorder may leave a person disabled in a wide range of normal human behaviors such as:

a. Disability relating to situational behavior.

b. Knowledge acquisition disability.

c. Occupational role disability.

Accommodation

a. Modification to the physical environment: Enclosed office or room dividers for privacy.

b. Schedule modification: Allow for rest periods following an attack; shift schedule to accommodate psychotherapy appointments.

c. Job modification: Eliminate secondary tasks that may contribute to panic attacks.

Generalized Anxiety Disorder F41.1

This name of this disorder suggests its main characteristic, which is a constant and unrealistic worry about matters such as finances or health. Persons with this condition may feel extremely restless and apprehensive. They may feel irritable, have headaches, and be unable to relax. Other symptoms include dizziness, rapid heartbeat, and insomnia.

Impairment

Individuals with this condition may have impairments of thinking and memory, and an inability to concentrate may exist if they are severely preoccupied. There may also be difficulties in following through with plans or instructions. On the other hand, the effect may be reduced when an individual is distracted, and workplace performance may not be affected at all in some people.

a. Impairment of thinking.

b. Impairment of memory.

c. Impairment of perception and attention.

d. Impairment of volition.

e. Impairment of behavior pattern.

Disability

a. Situation interpretation disability.

b. Disability in work routine.

c. Other severe behavior disorder.

Accommodation

Not much in the way of typical accommodations is helpful for people with this disorder. In some cases it might be helpful for a supervisor to make frequent inquiries and give reassurances. A schedule modification for psychotherapy may commonly be appropriate.

Obsessive-Compulsive Disorder F42

People who exhibit the milder characteristics of this disorder are highly desirable in the business community and are often counted among its highest achievers. To be designated as a disorder, the symptoms must be more severe and must be present on most days for at least two weeks and be a source of distress. The symptoms consist of distressing thoughts and/or actions that a person is unable to stop. People with this disorder are frequently depressed and occasionally may have panic attacks.

Impairment

Individuals may have a variety of impairments in thinking, including obsessional ideas and an inability to shift their focus from topic to topic because of their preoccupations. They may be inattentive, and their ability to concentrate on new assignments may be limited. They may also exhibit indecisiveness and a tendency toward repetitiveness.

a. Impairment of thinking.

b. Impairment of perception and attention.

c. Impairment of behavior pattern.

Disability

a. Self-awareness disability.

b. Personal safety disability.

c. Occupational role disability.

Accommodation

a. Job modification: Setting specific time limits on tasks to structure work habits and inhibit obsessions.

b. Schedule modification: Allow work at home to provide sufficient time to complete tasks.

Weekly or daily planning sessions with a supervisor to develop goals within specified time frames may provide structure and focus for an employee with this disorder. Working in a team situation may also provide structure, support a goal orientation, and provide distraction from obsessive thoughts or compulsive actions.

Reaction to Severe Stress, and Adjustment Disorders F43

These disorders are different from others because they are defined on the basis of causative factors in addition to symptoms. The causative influences include either a traumatic event that results in an acute stress reaction, or a change in life circumstances that produces long-lasting unpleasantness that leads to an adjustment disorder. The significance of a traumatic event or a change in life circumstances cannot be objectified. What may appear as insignificant to one person can be overwhelming for someone else. Individuals with these disorders almost always experience a negative impact on their social and/or work performance.

Acute Stress Reaction F43.0

This type of disorder is usually precipitated by a traumatic event such as an earthquake, criminal assault, or multiple losses such as the death of both parents. The connection between the event(s) and the onset of symptoms such as anxiety, depression, or withdrawal is immediate and clear. In the majority of cases, acute stress reactions resolve rapidly within a short period of time and are generally minimal after three days.

Impairment

An acute stress reaction may lead to either limited or almost total impairment of psychological functions. Most frequently noticed will be:

a. Impairment of thinking.

b. Impairment of wakefulness.

c. Impairment of perception and attention.

d. Impairment of volition.

e. Impairment of behavior pattern.

Disability

The disabilities associated with this disorder may be mild or severe and wide-ranging:

a. Family role disability.

b. Occupational role disability.

Accommodation

Schedule modification: The most appropriate accommodation for this condition is usually a short time off from work along with the suggestion to see a mental health professional even if the person can still perform the essential functions of his or her job. However, in some cases, it might be desirable that a person continue working; this should be evaluated on a case to case basis.

Since it is a temporary disorder by definition, it is unlikely that an acute stress reaction would even be covered under ADA. However, it would be prudent for an employer to be supportive and otherwise helpful in order to avoid adding to the problem and increasing the risk of a prolonged reaction that could turn into a disability.

Post-traumatic Stress Disorder F43.1

As in an acute stress reaction, people who are exposed to stressful events such as catastrophic disasters may react with delayed or prolonged symptoms such as anxiety, depression, and fear that the event will recur. They may also develop symptoms such as nightmares, insomnia, intrusive thoughts, and avoidant behavior. This reaction may start immediately after a traumatic event and continue indefinitely, or it may be delayed in some people as much as six months or longer.

Researchers have attempted to develop objective ratings of "traumatic events," but it is often the case that the meaning of an event differs from person to person and is therefore highly subjective. There are also many cases in which individuals have severe reactions to what might seem to be minor events. The reverse is also true.

Impairment

Impairment may include trouble concentrating, thinking, and sleeping. Detachment from other people may occur, and a person may be troubled by recurring intrusive memories, sometimes called flashbacks. People with post-traumatic stress disorder are generally very responsive to treatment. Possible impairments include:

a. Impairment of thinking.

b. Impairment of memory.

c. Impairment of attention.

d. Impairment of volition.

e. Impairment of behavior pattern.

Disability

a. Family role disability.

b. Occupational role disability.

Accommodation

Schedule modification: Allow for additional breaks or rest periods during the day.

Adjustment Disorders F43.2

During the period of adapting to significant life changes or the consequences of a stressful life event, an individual may experience an emotional disturbance that interfers with social and work functioning. The dysfunction usually manifests itself within one month of a stressor such as a serious medical illness and does not last longer than six months.

Impairment

As a consequence of the depressed mood and/or anxiety that accompanies this disorder, an individual may have the following impairments:

a. Impairment of thinking.

b. Impairment of attention and concentration.

c. Impairment of volition.

d. Impairment of behavior pattern.

Disability

The disabilities that accompany the impairments in this disorder are by definition temporary. However, if they extend beyond a six-month period the diagnosis is reevaluated and the disabilities should be considered as more long-term. Possible disabilities include:

a. Family role disability.
b. Occupational role disability.
c. Situational behavior disability.

Accommodation

Schedule modification: Arranging schedule so that an employee can go to psychotherapy.

Dissociative [Conversion] Disorders F44

This group of disorders is characterized by changes or disturbances in identity, memory, or consciousness that may have appeared either gradually or suddenly. They may be episodic or long-standing. Most types of dissociative states last only for brief periods up to several months, especially when connected to traumatic events. However, some amnestic states may last for years. Individuals with these disorders are rarely seen, and such disorders will probably either not affect work performance or fall outside of ADA.

Dissociative Amnesia F44.0

The primary characteristic of this disorder is usually a selective loss of memory that follows a traumatic event such as the unexpected death of a loved one or a wartime experience. This amnesia is either partial or complete.

Impairment

While the impairment of memory is primary, various emotional states may also result in additional impairments. For example, some individuals with dissociative amnesia are distressed and perplexed by their inability to remember, and this may cause anxiety along with difficulty in thinking and concentrating. Others, to the amazement of friends and family, may exhibit indifference to their amnesia.

a. Impairment of memory.

b. Impairment of thinking.

c. Impairment of attention and concentration.

d. Impairment of behavior pattern.

e. Impairment of volition.

Disability

a. Family role disability.

b. Occupational role disability.

Accommodation

In most cases the only accommodation necessary may be scheduling for psychotherapy. If there is emotional distress connected with the amnesia, it may be helpful to reduce or restructure nonessential job functions on the basis of the type and extent of disability.

Schedule modification: Shift schedule to accommodate therapy appointments.

Dissociative Fugue F44.1

In addition to the memory impairment that occurs in dissociative amnesia, this disorder is characterized by travel away from home and/or work with the person sometimes assuming a new identity. It is unlikely that this particular diagnosis will appear in a request for accommodation under ADA.

Dissociative Stupor F44.2

Individuals with this disorder are not likely to fall under the disability system, as it would be improbable that they would qualify for protection under ADA.

Trance and Possession Disorders F44.3

Individuals with this disorder are not likely to fall under the disability system, as it would be improbable that they would qualify for protection under ADA.

Dissociative Motor Disorders F44.4

Individuals with this disorder are not likely to fall under the disability system, as it would be improbable that they would qualify for protection under ADA.

Dissociative Convulsions F44.5

Individuals with this disorder are not likely to fall under the disability system, as it would be improbable that they would qualify for protection under ADA.

Dissociative Anaesthesia and Sensory Loss F44.6

Individuals with this disorder are not likely to fall under the disability system, as it would be improbable that they would qualify for protection under ADA.

Mixed Dissociative [Conversion] Disorders F44.7

These disorders are characterized by a mixed bag of symptoms that are associated with dissociative disorders but do not fit any of the clusters noted above.

Multiple Personality Disorder F44.81

This is a rare and highly controversial disorder, and the evidence for its existence is highly suspect. As with many other disorders, further research is necessary to examine the validity and reliability of multiple personality disorder. The type of impairments and associated disabilities are not specific enough to be delineated but could cover a wide range.

Somatoform Disorders F45

The primary characteristic of these disorders is repeated physical complaints without evidence of any medical disease or complaints that exceed in magnitude what would be expected for a particular medical problem. Attention seeking is frequently associated with these disorders.

Somatization Disorder F45.0

Many of these individuals have a long history (at least two years) of sometimes changing physical complaints before they are ultimately referred to a mental health professional for help. This is generally a chronic disorder and may cause many problems for friends, families, and co-workers. Reassurances from doctors that the symptoms do not have a physical basis do not have an effect.

Impairment

a. Impairment of thinking.

b. Impairment of attention and concentration.

c. Impairment of memory.

d. Impairment of volition.

e. Impairment of behavior pattern.

Disability

a. Personal safety disability.

b. Family role disability.

c. Occupational role disability.

Accommodation

a. Schedule modification: Additional breaks and/or schedule shift to attend psychotherapy.

b. Modification of physical environment: Provide a private work space to reduce unnecessary interactions with other employees.

Other Neurotic Disorders F48

Neurasthenia F48.0

The primary characteristic of this disorder is increasing fatigue that follows mental effort. This can manifest itself either in psychological complaints such as trouble concentrating or thinking, or in physical symptoms such as muscle weakness or pains. There can be overlap between the psychological and physical symptoms. There is controversy about whether or not this diagnosis is more suitable for those individuals who are being diagnosed with chronic fatigue syndrome. Many of the impairments are similar.

Impairment

a. Impairment of thinking.

b. Impairment of attention and concentration.

c. Impairment of volition.

d. Impairment of behavior pattern.

e. Impairment of wakefulness.

Disability

a. Disabilities of interpersonal relations.

b. Personal care disabilities.

c. Locomotor disabilities.

d. Occupational role disability.

Accommodation

a. Schedule modification: Allow for additional breaks or rest periods.

b. Job modification: Eliminate secondary tasks.

BEHAVIORAL SYNDROMES ASSOCIATED WITH PHYSIOLOGICAL DISTURBANCES AND PHYSICAL FACTORS F50-F59

Eating Disorders F50

Anorexia Nervosa F50.0

This is a well-publicized disorder that is exemplified by intentional weight loss, which is self-induced or maintained by vomiting, use of laxatives, excessive exercise, medications, or a combination of these. The disorder may be life threatening, although in many cases even spouses and close family members are not aware of the problem.

Impairment

a. Impairment of behavior pattern.

b. Impairment of volition.

c. Impairment of drives.

Disability

a. Family role disability.

b. Occupational role disability.

Accommodation

It is unlikely that most employees with this disorder will request or need an accommodation aside from a work schedule modification for therapy. There are many individuals with this disorder who nevertheless are able to perform their jobs satisfactorily.

Schedule modification: Shift schedule to attend psychotherapy sessions.

Bulimia Nervosa F50.2

Individuals with this disorder exhibit an ongoing preoccupation with food and periodically eat large amounts
within a short period of time. The overeating is followed by
the use of drugs, self-induced vomiting, or other methods
whose purpose is to prevent weight gain. This condition is
often accompanied by depression.

Impairment

a. Impairment of attention.

b. Impairment of emotion, affect, and mood.

c. Impairment of behavior pattern.

d. Impairment of drives.

Disability

a. Family role disability.

b. Occupational role disability.

Accommodation

Schedule modification: Shift schedule to accommodate
psychotherapy sessions.

Nonorganic Sleep Disorders F51

This group of disorders is characterized by a disturbance
in sleep that is due to emotional factors.

Nonorganic Insomnia F51.0

This is an ongoing condition in which the quantity and/or
quality of sleep is disturbed and is felt to be unsatisfactory
by the sufferers. It is often connected with stressful life

situations and itself may cause further distress as well as social and occupational dysfunction.

Impairment

a. Impairment of clarity of consciousness and the quality of conscious experience.

b. Impairment of attention.

c. Impairment of behavior pattern.

d. Impairment of psychomotor functions.

Disability

a. Family role disability.

b. Occupational role disability.

Accommodation

a. Schedule modification: Shift schedule for psychotherapy sessions; allow additional breaks or rest periods.

b. Job modification: Work at home or after hours.

Nonorganic Hypersomnia F51.1

A person with this condition may be excessively sleepy during the daytime, experience sleep attacks, or have a difficult time becoming fully awake. These symptoms are often associated with other diagnoses.

Impairment

a. Impairment of clarity of consciousness and the quality of conscious experience.

b. Impairment of attention.

c. Impairment of behavior pattern.

d. Impairment of psychomotor functions.

Disability

a. Family role disability.

b. Occupational role disability.

Accommodation

a. Physical environment modifications: Private office or room for naps.

b. Job modification: Allow work at home.

c. Schedule modification: Set own work schedule.

Nonorganic Disorder of the Sleep-Wake Schedule
F51.2

This diagnosis is characterized by the absence of a daily major sleep period. People with this problem may have several short sleep periods during a twenty-four hour day or may take frequent naps.

Impairment

a. Impairment of clarity of consciousness and the quality of conscious experience.

b. Impairment of attention.

c. Impairment of psychomotor functions.

Disability

a. Family role disability.

b. Occupational role disability.

Accommodation

a. Schedule modification: Additional breaks or rest periods; shift schedule for psychotherapy appointments.

b. Job modification: Work at home.

DISORDERS OF ADULT PERSONALITY AND BEHAVIOR F60-F69

These disorders are characterized by long-standing behavior patterns that generally begin by early adulthood and deviate from what is considered average behavior, thought, and feelings in a culture. Individuals with personality disorders are often but not always distressed by their symptoms. In some cases their behavior is more troublesome to others than to themselves.

The characteristics of many personality disorders are among the most studied of psychological conditions, and the names are often used by the general public to describe people. For example, we might say someone is passive-aggressive, or a sociopath.

Specific Personality Disorders F60

Paranoid Personality Disorder F60.0

The symptoms of this disorder include, among others, suspiciousness and a tendency to view the behavior of others as hostile.

Impairment

a. Impairment of thinking.

b. Impairment of perception.

c. Impairment of emotion.

d. Impairment of behavior pattern.

Disability

a. Disability in interpersonal relations.

b. Personal safety disability.

c. Disability relating to situational behavior.

d. Occupational role disability.

Accommodation

a. Changes in interpersonal communication: Self-appraisal by employee prior to feedback sessions with supervisor.

b. Physical environment modification: Private office to minimize interpersonal contact with other employees.

c. Schedule modification: Schedule shift for psychotherapy appointments.

Schizoid Personality Disorder F60.1

Individuals with this disorder are indifferent to social relationships and usually have no close friends aside from immediate relatives and/or a single confidant. These people are often seen as loners and may appear disinterested, aloof, and without emotion.

Impairment

a. Impairment of emotion, affect, and mood.

b. Impairment of volition.

c. Impairment of psychomotor functions.

d. Impairment of behavior pattern.

Disability

a. Disability in interpersonal relations.

b. Occupational role disability.

Accommodation

a. Changes in interpersonal communication: Allow for all or most work requests to be put in writing.

b. Job modification: Allow work to be done at home.

c. Schedule modification: Shift schedule to allow employee to attend psychotherapy appointments.

Dissocial (Antisocial) Personality Disorder F60.2

These individuals demonstrate a flagrant disregard for social norms and lack of concern for the feelings of others. They are typically irresponsible and do not maintain long-term intimate relationships even though they are extremely capable of meeting other people and forming new relationships. These individuals are prone to lying and to manipulating others to their own ends. They show no regard for safety and frequently fail to honor financial obligations and debts.

Impairment

a. Impairment of attention.

b. Impairment of drives.

c. Impairment of emotion, affect, and mood.

d. Impairment of volition.

e. Impairment of behavior pattern.

Disability

a. Self-awareness disability.

b. Disability relating to situational behavior.

c. Family role disability.

d. Occupational role disability.

e. Other behavior disability.

Accommodation

Individuals with this disorder may be very manipulative, and caution should be exercised in arranging any accommodations because of the possibility of lack of good faith.

They are generally not good candidates for psychotherapy and usually do not seek help on their own. The primary accommodation may be a highly structured and/or supervised environment.

- a. Schedule modification: Shift to accommodate psychotherapy appointments.
- b. Changes in interpersonal communication: Provide daily planning sessions along with close supervision.

Emotionally Unstable (Impulsive and Borderline)
Personality Disorder F60.3

This includes both impulsive and borderline types. While both are emotionally unstable, the impulsive type tends to behave without considering the consequences of the behavior and the borderline type is characterized by disturbances of self-image and intense fears of abandonment.

Impairment

- a. Impairment of perception.
- b. Impairment of attention.
- c. Impairment of drives.
- d. Impairment of emotion, affect, and mood.
- e. Impairment of volition.
- f. Impairment of behavior pattern.

Disability

- a. Self-awareness disability.
- b. Personal safety disability.
- c. Disability relating to situational behavior.
- d. Family role disability.

e. Occupational role disability.

f. Other behavior disability.

Accommodation

a. Changes in interpersonal communication: Provide positive feedback along with any negative appraisals.

b. Job modification: Work at home or eliminate secondary tasks that may be provocative.

c. Schedule modification: Shift schedule to accommodate psychotherapy sessions.

Histrionic Personality Disorder F60.4

Individuals diagnosed as histrionic are excessively emotional, although shallow, and seek reassurance and praise from others at the extreme. They tend to be very dramatic and attention seeking as well as flighty and prone to complaints of poor health.

Impairment

a. Impairment of thinking.

b. Impairment of perception.

c. Impairment of attention.

d. Impairment of drives.

e. Impairment of emotion, affect, and mood.

f. Impairment of volition.

g. Impairment of behavior pattern.

Disability

a. Personal safety disability.

b. Disability relating to situational behavior.

c. Family role disability.

d. Other behavior disability (indifference to accepted social standards).

Accommodation

a. Changes in interpersonal communication: Self-appraisal by employee before supervisor feedback occurs.

b. Schedule modification: Shift schedule to accommodate psychotherapy sessions.

Anakastic (Obsessive-Compulsive) Personality Disorder F60.5

This disorder is characterized by extreme rigidity and perfectionism, which often interfere with the completion of tasks. People with this disorder tend to value work to the exclusion of hobbies and personal relationships. They are often overly judgmental of others and tend to be extremely moralistic and conscientious.

Impairment

a. Impairment of flow and form of thought process.

b. Impairment of thought content.

c. Impairment of perception.

d. Impairment of attention.

e. Impairment of drives.

f. Impairment of emotion, affect, and mood.

g. Impairment of volition.

h. Impairment of behavior pattern.

Disability

a. Disability relating to situational behavior.

b. Family role disability.

c. Occupational role disability.

Accommodation

a. Changes in interpersonal communications: Schedule daily planning sessions along with hourly goals.

b. Schedule modification: Shift schedule to accommodate psychotherapy sessions.

Anxious [Avoidant] Personality Disorder F60.6

This disorder is characterized by the avoidance of social and/or work activities that require interpersonal interaction with others through fear of being criticized or rejected. Individuals with this disorder are tense and apprehensive and unwilling to become involved with others unless they are certain of being well regarded.

Impairment

a. Impairment of thought content.

b. Impairment of perception.

c. Impairment of attention.

d. Impairment of emotion, affect, and mood.

e. Impairment of volition.

f. Impairment of psychomotor functions.

g. Impairment of behavior pattern.

Disability

a. Disability relating to situational behavior.

b. Educational disability.

c. Family role disability.

d. Occupational role disability.

Accommodation

a. Changes in interpersonal communication: Schedule daily planning sessions.

b. Modification to physical environment: Allow work at home and/or provide room dividers or private office. Reduce secondary tasks involving interpersonal activities.

c. Schedule modification: Shift schedule to accommodate psychotherapy sessions.

d. Job modification: Work at home.

Habit and Impulse Disorders F63

These problems may be symptoms of other disorders, or they may appear to be self-contained disorders. The main characteristic is a repetitive pattern of behavior that has destructive potential for the individual and others.

Pathological Gambling F63.0

This disorder is characterized by frequent episodes of gambling to the detriment of social and work activities. Gambling often leads to destructive consequences and is not affected by the adversity it causes.

Impairment

a. Impairment of flow and form of thought processes.

b. Impairment of thought content.

c. Impairment of attention.

Disability

a. Family role disability.

b. Occupational role disability.

c. Other behavior disability.

Accommodation

Schedule modification: Shift schedule to accommodate psychotherapy sessions.

Pathological Fire-Setting [Pyromania] F63.1

Currently not covered under ADA.

Pathological Stealing [Kleptomania] F63.2

Currently not covered under ADA.

Gender Identity Disorders F64

Transsexualism F64.0

Currently not covered under ADA.

Dual-Role Transvestism F64.1

Currently not covered under ADA.

Disorders of Sexual Preference F65

Fetishism F65.0

Currently not covered under ADA.

Fetishistic Transvestism F65.1

Currently not covered under ADA.

Exhibitionism F65.2

Currently not covered under ADA.

Voyeurism F65.3

Currently not covered under ADA.

Paedophilia F65.4

Currently not covered under ADA.

Sadomasochism F65.5

Currently not covered under ADA.

Other Disorders of Adult Personality and Behavior F68

Elaboration of Physical Symptoms for Psychological Reasons F68.0

The primary characteristic of this disorder is the prolonging and exaggerating of physical symptoms that originated from a legitimate illness or injury. There is preoccupation with symptoms, and doctor shopping is frequent. At times there is a clear motivation for financial gain; this disorder is also called compensation neurosis.

Impairment

a. Impairment of flow and form of thought processes.

b. Impairment of thought content.

c. Impairment of attention.

d. Impairment of emotion, affect, and mood.

e. Impairment of volition.

f. Impairment of behavior pattern.

Disability

a. Disability relating to situational behavior.

b. Family role disability.

c. Occupational role disability.

d. Other behavior disability.

Accommodation

Schedule modification: Shift schedule to accommodate psychotherapy sessions.

MENTAL RETARDATION F70-F79

Mental retardation (MR) is a condition that manifests itself during development and is characterized by a wide range and degree of impairments in motor, cognitive, language, and social skills. In many cases the cause of MR may be unknown, and other mental disorders may also be present. The occurrence of additional mental disorders in the MR population is higher than in the general population.

MR defines a wide range of individuals with differing impairments and abilities. Businesses that actively recruit and employ the mentally retarded can usually place them in jobs that are best suited for their ability levels. Separate diagnostic categories need not be listed for the purposes of this book.

Impairment

a. Intellectual impairments.

b. Impairment of memory.

c. Impairment of flow and form of thought processes.

d. Other intellectual impairment.

e. Impairment of consciousness and the quality of conscious experience.

f. Impairment of perception.

g. Impairment of attention.

h. Impairment of emotions, affect, and mood.

i. Impairment of volition.

j. Impairment of psychomotor functions.

k. Impairment of behavior pattern.

Disability

a. Self-awareness disability.

b. Disability relating to location in time and space.

c. Personal safety disability.

d. Disability relating to situational behavior.

e. Knowledge acquisition disability.

f. Other educational disability.

g. Family role disability.

h. Occupational role disability.

i. Other behavior disability.

Accommodation

a. Changes in interpersonal communication.

b. Modifications to physical environment.

c. Job modification.

d. Schedule modification.

SCHIZOPHRENIA, SCHIZOTYPAL AND DELUSIONAL DISORDERS F20-F29

Schizophrenia F20

Schizophrenia refers to a condition that is generally characterized by sometimes bizarre symptoms such as delusions and hallucinations. However, there is no particular symptom that positively identifies someone as schizophrenic, and the diagnostic criteria have changed over the years. There are many common myths, fears, and stereotypes that the general public tends to associate with the diagnosis of schizophrenia; I have covered many of these in Chapter 1.

Schizophrenia has at various times been viewed as a disease, an illness, or a disorder. There is no scientific consensus regarding the cause of this condition, nor is there any conclusive evidence that it is genetically or otherwise caused by physical factors. The diagnosis is often problematic and, as with other conditions, there may be a wide range of opinions in any particular case.

The onset of this condition is, in retrospect, often preceded by a period of time during which there are increasing changes in behavior, such as at school and work. Personal habits may deteriorate, while friends, family, and co-workers may notice increasingly bizarre behavior.

Impairment

a. Impairment of flow and form of thought processes.

b. Impairment of thought content.

c. Impairment of clarity of consciousness and the quality of conscious experience.

d. Impairment of perception.

e. Impairment of attention.

f. Impairment of drives.

g. Impairment of emotion, affect, and mood.

h. Impairment of volition.

i. Impairment of psychomotor functions.

j. Impairment of behavior pattern.

Disability

a. Self-awareness disability.

b. Personal safety disability.

c. Disability relating to situational behavior.

d. Knowledge acquisition disability.

e. Family role disability.

f. Occupational role disability.

g. Other behavior disability.

Accommodation

a. Changes in interpersonal communication: Arranging for all work requests to be put in writing and/or requesting self-appraisal prior to feedback from supervisor.

b. Modification to physical environment: Enclosed office to reduce distractions.

c. Job modification: Work at home.

d. Schedule modification: Shift schedule to accommodate psychotherapy sessions.

Schizotypal Disorder F21

This disorder is characterized by many of the behaviors and thinking that resemble the symptoms of schizophrenia. An individual with this condition may eventually develop schizophrenia, or the course of the disorder may be chronic.

Impairment

a. Impairment of flow and form of thought processes.

b. Impairment of thought content.

c. Impairment of clarity of consciousness and the quality of conscious experience.

d. Impairment of perception.

e. Impairment of attention.

f. Impairment of drives.

g. Impairment of emotion, affect, and mood.

h. Impairment of volition.

i. Impairment of psychomotor functions.

j. Impairment of behavior pattern.

Disability

a. Self-awareness disability.

b. Personal safety disability.

c. Disability relating to situational behavior.

d. Knowledge acquisition disability.

e. Family role disability.

f. Occupational role disability.

g. Other behavior disability.

Accommodation

a. Changes in interpersonal communication: Arranging for all work requests to be put in writing and/or requesting self-appraisal prior to feedback from supervisor.

b. Modification to physical environment: Enclosed office to reduce distractions.

c. Job modification: Work at home.

d. Schedule modification: Shift schedule to accommodate psychotherapy sessions.

Persistent Delusional Disorders F22

Delusional Disorders F22.0

A person with this disorder has a delusion or delusions that persist, and the condition is sometimes lifelong. The delusions may cause minor or major conflicts with others, and they are usually resistant to evidence to the contrary.

Impairment

a. Impairment of flow and form of thought processes.

b. Impairment of thought content.

   c. Impairment of clarity of consciousness and the quality of conscious experience.

   d. Impairment of perception.

   e. Impairment of attention.

   f. Impairment of drives.

   g. Impairment of emotion, affect, and mood.

   h. Impairment of volition.

   i. Impairment of psychomotor functions.

   j. Impairment of behavior pattern.

Disability

   a. Self-awareness disability.

   b. Personal safety disability.

   c. Disability relating to situational behavior.

   d. Knowledge acquisition disability.

   e. Family role disability.

   f. Occupational role disability.

   g. Other behavior disability.

Accommodation

   a. Changes in interpersonal communication: Arranging for all work requests to be put in writing and/or requesting self-appraisal prior to feedback from supervisor.

   b. Modification to physical environment: Enclosed office to reduce distractions.

   c. Job modification: Work at home.

   d. Schedule modification: Shift schedule to accommodate psychotherapy sessions.

Acute and Transient Psychotic Disorders F23

This group of disorders is characterized by brief psychotic episodes that usually require hospitalization. Persons affected are eligible for disability during the time they are incapacitated and can generally return to work with little or no effect on their performance. These individuals are usually excellent employees who are only temporarily unable to do their work.

Impairment

a. Impairment of flow and form of thought processes.

b. Impairment of thought content.

c. Impairment of clarity of consciousness and the quality of conscious experience.

d. Impairment of perception.

e. Impairment of attention.

f. Impairment of drives.

g. Impairment of emotion, affect, and mood.

h. Impairment of volition.

i. Impairment of psychomotor functions.

j. Impairment of behavior pattern.

Disability

a. Self-awareness disability.

b. Personal safety disability.

c. Disability relating to situational behavior.

d. Knowledge acquisition disability.

e. Family role disability.

f. Occupational role disability.

g. Other behavior disability.

Accommodation

a. Changes in interpersonal communication: Reassurance from supervisor following hospitalization.
b. Schedule modification: Shift schedule to accommodate psychotherapy sessions.

Schizoaffective Disorders F25

Impairments, disabilities, and accommodations are similar to other psychotic disorders.

MOOD [AFFECTIVE] DISORDERS F30-F39

Impairments, disabilities, and accommodations are similar to other psychotic disorders.

Manic Episode F30

Impairments, disabilities, and accommodations are similar to other psychotic disorders.

Bipolar Affective Disorder F31

This disorder is characterized by episodes of severe mood swings during which an individual is alternately deeply depressed at one extreme and highly active and energized at the other end of the spectrum. During the time interval separating the two poles of the disorder, an individual with this condition may show no evidence of the disturbed phases, which may also include psychotic symptoms. There are numerous subgroups of the disorder depending upon the presence of mania and/or depression, with or without psychotic symptoms. It is not necessary to describe each of these for the purposes of this book.

Impairment

a. Impairment of thinking.

b. Impairment of consciousness and wakefulness.

c. Impairments of perception, attention, and concentration.

d. Impairment of emotive and volitional functions.

e. Impairment of behavior pattern.

Disability

a. Self-awareness disability.

b. Personal safety disability.

c. Disability relating to situational behavior.

d. Disabilities in interpersonal relations.

Accommodation

a. Changes in interpersonal communication: Train a supervisor to provide support and positive feedback to an employee who has returned from a hospitalization.

b. Schedule modification: Shift schedule to accommodate phychotherapy sessions.

c. Job modification: Allow work at home.

Depressive Episode F32

Depressive episodes can range from mild to severe with varying degrees of functional impairment. Hospitalization may be required in the more severe cases with psychotic symptoms.

Impairment

a. Impairment of thinking.

b. Impairment of consciousness and wakefulness.

c. Impairments of perception, attention, and concentration.

d. Impairment of emotive and volitional functions.

e. Impairment of behavior pattern.

Disability

a. Self-awareness disability.

b. Personal safety disability.

c. Disability relating to situational behavior.

d. Disabilities in interpersonal relations.

Accommodation

a. Changes in interpersonal communication: Train a supervisor to provide support and positive feedback to an employee who has returned from a hospitalization.

b. Schedule modification: Shift schedule to accommodate psychotherapy sessions.

c. Job modification: Allow work at home.

Recurrent Depressive Disorder F33

This disorder is also characterized by a range of severity, with the onset of the first episode occurring later in life.

Impairment

a. Impairment of thinking.

b. Impairment of consciousness and wakefulness.

c. Impairments of perception, attention, and concentration.

d. Impairment of emotive and volitional functions.

e. Impairment of behavior pattern.

Disability

a. Self-awareness disability.

b. Personal safety disability.

c. Disability relating to situational behavior.

d. Disabilities in interpersonal relations.

Accommodation

a. Changes in interpersonal communication: Train a supervisor to provide support and positive feedback to an employee who has returned from a hospitalization.

b. Schedule modification: Shift schedule to accommodate psychotherapy sessions.

c. Job modification: Allow work at home.

Persistent Mood [Affective] Disorders F34

These disorders of mood often last for years or exist over the lifetime of an individual.

Cyclothymia F34.0

This disorder usually develops early in life and is characterized by fluctuating periods of mild depression and mild elation. In general, the disorder may have a minimal impact on functioning, and individuals with this condition usually do not experience too much of a decline in their work performance.

Impairment

a. Impairment of thinking.

b. Impairment of consciousness and wakefulness.

c. Impairments of perception, attention, and concentration.

d. Impairment of emotive and volitional functions.

e. Impairment of behavior pattern.

Disability

a. Self-awareness disability.

b. Personal safety disability.

c. Disability relating to situational behavior.

d. Disabilities in interpersonal relations.

Accommodation

Schedule modification: Shift schedule to accommodate psychotherapy sessions.

Dysthymia F34.1

This disorder is characterized by a long-standing and chronic depressive mood that lifts only for occasional brief periods of time, if at all. As in cyclothymia, this disorder generally does not result in impairments severe enough to significantly affect work performance.

Impairment

a. Impairment of thinking.

b. Impairment of consciousness and wakefulness.

c. Impairments of perception, attention, and concentration.

d. Impairment of emotive and volitional functions.

e. Impairment of behavior pattern.

Disability

a. Self-awareness disability.

b. Personal safety disability.

c. Disability relating to situational behavior.

d. Disabilities in interpersonal relations.

Accommodation

Schedule modification: Shift schedule to accommodate psychotherapy sessions.

The foregoing are the major examples of disorders and possible accommodations that might reasonably be made for each. I want to reemphasize that each case must be evaluated independently and that there are, for the most part, no general rules for making decisions about what might make for a reasonable accommodation.

If employees feel safe in stepping forward and asking for help under ADA, it is not going to be all that difficult or costly to make the kinds of accommodations that would, in my estimation, satisfy the intent of the law and make it possible for these people to work. It will certainly be much less costly than the accommodations necessitated by many physical disabilities.

Regardless of how well a company complies with ADA, it is not inconceivable that requests for accommodations might be made that are not in good faith. If it is suspected that this is the case, businesses should be aware that they can defend themselves against such requests. If it is suspected that either a request or a recommendation is not in good faith, you should obtain a second opinion from a mental health professional who has had experience in evaluating and challenging psychological testimony in legal cases.

7

Americans with "Mental" Disabilities Act of 1990

John H. Feldmann III and Maria C. Brandt

INTRODUCTION

The Americans with Disabilities Act ("ADA" or the "Act"), P.L. 101-336, 104 Stat. 327, 42 U.S.C. § 12101 et seq., was signed by President George Bush on July 26, 1990. Title I, which covers employment of individuals with a disability, became effective twenty-four months after the date it was signed—that is, on July 26, 1992. For the first two years after its effective date, the ADA will apply to all employers (except the United States and bona fide private membership clubs) who have twenty-five or more employees. After two years, the law covers employers with fifteen or more employees.

OVERVIEW OF THE ADA

The ADA is divided into five sections. Title I covers private-sector employment. Title II applies (1) to state and local governments and their instrumentalities (both as employers and as providers of service to the public), and (2) to transportation entities operated by state or local governments or their instrumentalities. Title III covers private-sector public accommodations and private entities operating public transportation services. Title IV addresses telecommunication relay services. Title V contains various miscellaneous provisions.

This discussion will focus on Title I of the ADA, which covers employment discrimination against individuals with disabilities, and the regulations under Title I. It also emphasizes mental disability issues in its examples.

PROHIBITED EMPLOYMENT DISCRIMINATION UNDER THE ADA

Title I prohibits employers from discriminating against a qualified individual with a disability because of the person's disability in regard to job application procedures, hiring, advancement, or discharge of employees, employee compensation, job training, and other terms, conditions, and privileges of employment. 42 U.S.C. § 12112(a).

The ADA defines "discriminate" to include (1) classifying a job applicant or employee in a way that adversely affects the opportunities or status of the applicant or employee; (2) participating in a contract that has the effect of subjecting a qualified applicant or employee with a disability to discrimination; (3) utilizing a standard, criteria, or methods of administration that have the effect of discrimination on the basis of disability, or that perpetuate the discrimination of others who are subject to common administrative control; (4) excluding or otherwise denying equal jobs or benefits to a qualified individual because of the known disability of an individual with whom the qualified individual is known to have a relationship or association; (5) not making reasonable accommodations to the known limitations of an otherwise qualified applicant or employee with a disability unless the covered entity can demonstrate that the accommodation would impose an undue hardship; (6) using qualification standards or tests that screen out an individual with a disability or a class of individuals with disabilities unless the standard is shown to be job related for the position in question and is consistent with business necessity; and (7) failing to select and administer tests concerning employment in the most effective manner to ensure that, when a test is administered to a job applicant or employee who has a disability that impairs sensory, manual, or speaking skills, the test results accurately reflect the skills, aptitude, or whatever other factor of such applicant or employee that the test purports to measure, rather than reflecting the impaired sensory, manual, or speaking skills of the employee or applicant (except where such skills are the factors that the test purports to measure). *See* 42 U.S.C. § 12112(b). The ADA also limits the use of medical examinations; see discussion below.

DEFINITIONS OF ADA TERMS

Disability/Physical or Mental Impairment

For all sections of the ADA, the term "disability" is defined to have three meanings. First, a disability is "[a] physical or mental impairment that substantially limits one or more of the major life activities of such individual." 42 U.S.C. § 12102(2)(A). The regulations define mental disabilities as follows: "any mental or psychological disorder, such as mental retardation, organic brain syndrome, emotional or mental illness, and specific learning disabilities." 29 C.F.R. § 1630.2(h)(2).

Specifically excluded from the Act's definition of disability are homosexuality; bisexuality; transvestism; pedophilia; transsexualism; exhibitionism; voyeurism; pyromania; compulsive gambling; kleptomania; gender identity disorders not resulting from physical impairments or other sexual behavior disorders; and psychoactive substance use disorders resulting from current illegal use of drugs. 42 U.S.C. § 12211; 29 C.F.R. § 1630.3(d).

Congress adopted the definition of a disability from the Rehabilitation Act of 1973, 29 U.S.C. § 791 et seq., definition of the term 'individual with a handicap.' "By doing so, Congress intended that the relevant caselaw developed under the Rehabilitation Act be generally applicable to the term 'disability' as used in the ADA." Appendix to 29 C.F.R. Part 1630—Interpretive Guidance on Title I of the Americans with Disabilities Act ("Interpretive Guidance") discussion for Section 1630.2(g).[1]

It is important to distinguish, however, between conditions that are truly impairments and physical, psychological, environmental, cultural, and economic characteristics that are not impairments. For example, the definition of "impairment" does not include "common personality traits such as poor judgment or a quick temper where these are not symptoms of a mental or psychological disorder." Interpretive Guidance discussion for Section 1630.2(h).

Second, a disability is defined to include individuals who have a history of or have been misclassified as having an impairment. 42 U.S.C. § 12102(2)(B). This provision is included in the definition in part to protect individuals who have recovered from a physical or mental impairment which previously substantially limited them in a major life activity. Examples of the first group (those who have a history of an impairment) are persons with histories of mental or emotional illness, or a learning disability; examples of the second group (those who have been misclassified as having a psychopathic impairment) are persons who have been misclassified as mentally retarded. *See* Interpretive Guidance discussion for Section 1630.2(k). Other examples are explained in the E.E.O.C. Technical Assistance Manual on the Employment Provision (Title I) of the Americans with Disabilities Act, January 1992 ("Technical Assistance Manual"):

—A job applicant formerly was a patient at a state institution. When very young she was misdiagnosed as being psychopathic and this misdiagnosis was never removed from her records. If this person is otherwise qualified for a job, and an employer does not hire her based on this record, the employer has violated the ADA.

—A person who has a learning disability applies for a job as secretary/receptionist. The employer reviews records from a previous employer indicating that he was labeled as "mentally retarded." Even though the person's resume shows that he meets all requirements for the job, the employer does not interview him because he doesn't want to hire a person who has mental retardation. This employer has violated the ADA.

—A job applicant was hospitalized for treatment for cocaine addiction several years ago. He has been successfully rehabilitated and has not engaged in the illegal use of drugs since receiving treatment. This applicant has a record of an impairment that substantially limited his major life activities. If he is qualified to perform a job, it would be discriminatory to reject him based on the record of his former addiction. (Technical Assistance Manual § 2.2(b))

Third, a disability is defined to include individuals who are regarded as having an impairment. 42 U.S.C. § 12102(2)(C). This part of the definition protects people who are "perceived" as having disabilities from employment decisions based on stereotypes, fears, or misconceptions about disability. "It applies to decisions based on unsubstantiated concerns about productivity, safety, insurance, liability, attendance, costs of accommodation, accessibility, workers' compensation costs or acceptance by co-workers and customers." Technical Assistance Manual § 2.2(c).

Substantially Limited with Respect to Major Life Activities

Major life activities means functions like caring for one-self, performing manual tasks, walking, seeing, hearing, speaking, breathing, learning, and working. 29 C.F.R. § 1630.2(i). According to the regulations for Title I, "substantially limits" means (1) unable to perform a major life activity that the average person in the general population can perform; or (2) significantly restricted as to the condition, manner, or duration under which an individual can perform a particular major life activity as compared to the condition, manner, or duration under which the average person in the general population can perform that same major life activity. 29 C.F.R. § 1630.2(j)(1).

The regulations cite several factors that should be considered in making the determination of whether an impairment is substantially limiting. These factors are (1) the nature and severity of the impairment; (2) the duration or expected duration of the impairment; and (3) the permanent or long-term impact, or the expected permanent or long-term impact of or resulting from the impairment. 29 C.F.R. § 1630.2(j)(2).

An individual who is not substantially limited with respect to any other major life activity may be substantially limited with respect to the major life activity of working. The regulations state that, with respect to working, the term "substantially limits" means significantly restricted in the ability to perform either a class of jobs or a broad range of jobs in various classes as compared to the average person having comparable training, skills, and abilities. The inability to perform a single, particular job will not constitute a substantial limitation in the major life activity of working under the ADA. 29 C.F.R. § 1630.2(j)(3).

Qualified Individuals with a Disability

Applicants or employees are covered by the Act where they are "qualified" for the job in question. A "qualified individual with a disability" is someone with a disability who, with or without reasonable accommodation, can perform the essential functions of the job that the individual holds or desires because he or she has the requisite skill, experience, and education requirements. 42 U.S.C. § 12102(8); 29 C.F.R. § 1630.2(m).

If the individual rejects a reasonable accommodation that is necessary to enable him or her to perform the essential functions of the position held or desired, and cannot as a result of the rejection perform the essential functions of the position, the individual will not be considered a qualified individual with a disability. 29 C.F.R. § 1630.9(d).

This includes individuals who have been successfully rehabilitated and are no longer using drugs or are currently participating in a rehabilitation program and are no longer engaging in the use of illegal drugs, as well as persons erroneously regarded as using illegal drugs but who do not engage in that use. Current drug users are not protected. 42 U.S.C. § 12114(b); 29 C.F.R. § 1630.3(b).

Although alcoholics may be included as qualified individuals with a disability, they are not protected under the Act if they use alcohol, or are under the influence of alcohol, at the workplace. 42 U.S.C. § 12114(g); 29 C.F.R. § 1630.3(a).

Essential Job Functions

"Essential functions" means primary job duties that are intrinsic to the employment position the individual holds or desires. The term does not refer to those positions that are marginal or peripheral functions of the position. 29 C.F.R. § 1630.2(n).

Reasonable Accommodations

Employers are required to provide reasonable accommodations to qualified employees or applicants with disabilities. 42 U.S.C. § 12112(b)(5); 29 C.F.R. § 1630.9(a). The regulations describe three categories of reasonable accommodation: (1) accommodations that are required to ensure equal opportunity in the application process; (2) accommodations that enable the employer's employees with disabilities to perform the essential functions of the position held or desired; and (3) accommodations that enable the employer's employees with disabilities to enjoy the same benefits and privileges of employment as are enjoyed by employees without disabilities. 29 C.F.R. § 1630.2(o)(1).

The ADA and the regulations list examples of the most common types of accommodation that an employer may be required to provide. This listing, however, is not exhaustive. It includes:

1. Making existing facilities used by employees readily accessible to and usable by individuals with disabilities.

2. Reasonable accommodation may also include job restructuring; part-time or modified work schedules; reassignment to a vacant position; acquisition or modification of equipment or devices; appropriate adjustment or modifications of examinations, training materials, or policies; and the provision of qualified readers and interpreters. (29 C.F.R. § 1630.2(o)(2))

An example of a reasonable accommodation in the testing process is:

An applicant who has dyslexia, which causes difficulty in reading, should be given an oral rather than a written test, unless reading is an essential function of the job. Or, an individual with a visual disability or a learning disability might be allowed more time to take a test, unless the test is designed to measure speed required on a job. (Technical Assistance Manual § 3.10(7))

An employer is allowed to conduct pre-employment job testing which screens out individuals with certain disabilities where the testing criteria are job-related. For example:

A person with dyslexia should be given an opportunity to take a written test orally, if the dyslexia seriously impairs the individual's ability to read. But if ability to read is a job-related function that the test is designed to measure, the employer could require that a person with dyslexia take the written test. However, even in this situation, reasonable accommodation should be considered. The person with dyslexia might be accommodated with a reader, unless the ability to read unaided is an essential job function, unless such an accommodation would not be possible on the job for which s/he is being tested, or would be an undue hardship. For example, the ability to read without help would be essential for a proofreader's job. Or, a dyslexic firefighter applicant might be disqualified if he could not quickly read necessary instructions for dealing with specific toxic substances at the site of a fire when no reader would be available.

Providing extra time to take a test may be a reasonable accommodation for people with certain disabilities, such as visual impairments, learning disabilities, or mental retardation. On the other hand, an employer could require that an applicant complete a test within an established time frame if speed is one of the skills that the test is designed to measure. However, the results of a timed test should not be used to exclude a person with a disability, unless the test measures a *particular* speed necessary to perform an essential function of the job, and there is no reasonable accommodation that would enable this person to perform that function within prescribed time frames, or the accommodation would cause an undue hardship. (Technical Assistance Manual § 5.6(2); emphasis in original)

Examples of reasonable accommodations with respect to individuals with mental disabilities on the job include the following:

A person who has a disability that makes it difficult to write might be allowed to computerize records that have been maintained manually.

A person with mental retardation who can perform job tasks but has difficulty remembering the order in which to do the tasks might be provided with a list to check off each task; the checklist could be reviewed by a supervisor at the end of the day. (Technical Assistance Manual § 3.10(2)).

As another example, a simple cardboard form, called a "jig," may make it possible for a person with mental retardation to properly fold jeans as a stock clerk in a retail store. This accommodation would cost the employer nothing. Technical Assistance Manual § 3.10(6).

Also, it may be a reasonable accommodation to allow more time for training or to provide extra assistance to people with learning disabilities or people with mental impairments. Technical Assistance Manual § 3.10(7).

A reasonable accommodation for job training might include materials in accessible formats and/or readers for people with learning disabilities, and for people with mental retardation. Technical Assistance Manual § 7.6.

Undue Hardship

Reasonable accommodations must be provided to the extent they do not cause "undue hardship." 42 U.S.C. § 12112(b)(5)(A); 29 C.F.R. § 1630.9(a). The term means an action requiring *significant difficulty or expense*, when considered in light of numerous factors. 29 C.F.R. § 1630.2(p)(1). The factors to be considered in determining whether a particular accommodation would cause "undue hardship" include the nature and cost of the accommodation needed, the overall financial resources of the site or sites involved in the provision of the reasonable accommodation, taking into account the number of employees at the site and the accommodation's impact on the facility; the overall resources of the entity, taking into account its overall size, the number of employees, and the number, type, and location of its facilities; the type of operation or operations of the covered entity, including the composition of its workforce and the relationship of the site or sites in question to the covered entity; and the impact of the accommodation upon the operation of the site, including the impact on the ability of other employees to perform their duties and the impact on the site's ability to conduct business. 29 C.F.R. § 1630.2(p)(2).

Another factor to be considered is the availability of outside funding to pay for accommodations. Such funding may be available from state vocational rehabilitation agencies, or through federal, state, or local tax deductions or tax credits. 29 C.F.R. § 1630.2(p)(2)(i); Interpretive Guidance discussion of Section 1630.2(p). For example, one type of accommodation could include the use of a job coach for people with mental retardation and other disabilities who benefit from individualized on-the-job training and services provided at no cost by vocational rehabilitation agencies in "supported employment" programs. Technical Assistance Manual § 3.10(10).

In addition, even where an entity is not required to pay for an accommodation because it would cause undue hardship, the entity cannot refuse to hire a qualified applicant where the applicant is willing to make his or her own arrangements for the provision of such accommodation. Interpretive Guidance discussion of Section 1630.2(p).

Excessive cost is only one of the several possible bases upon which an employer might be able to demonstrate an undue hardship. Another would be that the accommodation is unduly disruptive to other employees or to the functioning of the business. Interpretive Guidance discussion of Section 1630.2(p).

Employers are obligated to make reasonable accommodation only to the physical or mental limitation of a qualified individual with a disability that is known to the employer. If an employee with a known disability is having difficulty performing his or her job, an employer may inquire whether the employee is in need of a reasonable accommodation. In general, however, it is the responsibility of the individual with a disability to inform the employer that an accommodation is needed. *See* Interpretive Guidance discussion of Section 1630.9. In addition, according to the Technical Assistance Manual, an employer may ask for written documentation from a doctor, psychologist, or other professional with knowledge of the person's functional limitations. Technical Assistance Manual Section 3.6.

By including in the ADA a number of factors to be considered in determining undue hardship, Congress intended to fashion a flexible approach. The process of determining the appropriate reasonable accommodation is an informal, interactive, problem solving technique involving both the employer and the qualified individual with a disability. Interpretive Guidance discussion of Section 1630.9.

If more than one accommodation will enable the individual to perform the essential functions, the preference of the individual with a disability should be given primary consideration. However, the employer providing the accommodation has the ultimate discretion to choose between effective accommodations, and may choose the less expensive accommodation or the accommodation that is easier for it to provide. Interpretive Guidance discussion of Section 1630.9.

THE ADA AND MEDICAL EXAMINATIONS

Pre-employment and Pre-offer

Before a job offer, the employer may not conduct any medical examination or make any inquiries of an applicant about whether the applicant has a disability. The employer may, however, inquire into the ability of an applicant to perform job-related functions. 42 U.S.C. § 12112(d)(2); 29 C.F.R. §§ 1630.13(a), 1630.14(a). For example, an employer may not ask if a potential employee has ever been treated for a mental condition or if an employee is taking any prescribed drugs. (Questions about use of prescription drugs are not permitted before a conditional job offer, because the answers to such questions might reveal the existence of certain disabilities which require prescribed medication.) Technical Assistance Manual § 5.5(b).

A test to determine the illegal use of drugs is not considered a medical examination under the ADA. 42 U.S.C. § 12114(d); 29 C.F.R. § 1630.16(c)(1). However, the regulations note that this exemption should not encourage or authorize an employer to conduct drug tests of applicants or employees or to make employment decisions based on those test results. 29 C.F.R. § 1630.16(c)(1).

Pre-employment and Post-offer

After a job offer has been made to an applicant and before the applicant starts work, an employer may require a medical examination and may condition an offer on the results of the examination if all entering employees in a particular job category are subjected to an examination and if the information obtained is collected and maintained separately from other personnel records and is treated as confidential. 42 U.S.C. § 12112(d)(3); 29 C.F.R. § 1630.14(b)(1). The regulations state that these medical exams do not have to be job-related and consistent with business necessity. However, if certain criteria are used to screen out an employee or employees with disabilities as a result of an examination or inquiry, the exclusionary criteria must be job-related and consistent with business necessity, and performance of the essential job functions cannot be accomplished with reasonable accommodation. 29 C.F.R. § 1630.14(b)(3).

During Employment

Once an individual is employed, the employer may not conduct a medical examination or make inquiries of an employee about whether the employee is an individual with a disability or about the nature or severity of the disability, unless the examination or inquiry "is shown to be job-related and consistent with business necessity." 42 U.S.C. § 12112(d)(4); 29 C.F.R. § 1630.14(c).

An employer need not hire or retain an individual who poses a "direct threat" to the health or safety of other individuals in the workplace. 29 C.F.R. §§ 1630.15(b)(2), 1630.16(e). A direct threat means a significant risk to the health or safety of others that cannot be eliminated by reasonable accommodation; for example, an employer would not have to hire a person with active, contagious tuberculosis. *See* 42 U.S.C. § 12111(3); 29 C.F.R. § 1630.2(r); *see also* CDC Listing of Diseases Transmitted Through Food Supply, dated August 9, 1991. A person with a mental disability may also be found to pose a direct threat to the health and safety of others. In *Doe v. Region 13 Mental Health-Mental Retardation Commission*, 704 F.2d 1402, 1410 (5th Cir. 1983), the employer was allowed to place a psychiatric worker on leave of absence where the worker threatened to commit suicide, and the employer determined, based on expert opinion, that she might pass on this concept to her patients. The determination that an individual poses a "direct threat" shall be based "on an individualized assessment of the individual's present ability to safely perform the essential functions of the job." 29 C.F.R. § 1630.2(r).

THE ADA AND INSURANCE

One of the issues Congress addressed in the ADA was how the ADA will affect insurance practices. Congress did not intend the ADA to be construed to restrict various insurance practices on the part of insurance companies and employers, as long as those practices are not used to evade the purposes of the Act. *See* Interpretive Guidance discussion of Section 1630.16(f).

It is legal—at least according to the bill's legislative history—to offer an insurance policy that limits coverage for certain procedures or treatments—for example, a limit on kidney dialysis, or the number of blood transfusions. However, it is not permissible to deny coverage to those individuals for other procedures or treatments. Further, the limitations must apply to all employees, with or without disabilities. *See* Interpretive Guidance discussion of Section 1630.5.

Also, with respect to group health insurance coverage, an individual with a preexisting condition may be denied coverage for that condition for the period specified in the policy but cannot be denied coverage for illness or injuries unrelated to the preexisting condition. The intent of the bill is that the employee benefit plans should not be found to be in violation of the ADA under disparate impact analysis simply because they do not address the special needs of every person with a disability, such as additional sick leave or medical coverage. *See* Interpretive Guidance discussion of Section 1630.5.

NOTE

1. The following types of mental disabilities have been determined to fall within the definition of "handicap" under the Rehabilitation Act: depressive neurosis (including suicidal tendencies) (*Doe v. Region 13 Mental Health-Mental Retardation Commission,* 704 F.2d 1402 (5th Cir. 1983)); drug and alcohol addiction (*Gallagher v. Catto,* 778 F.Supp. 570 (D.D.C. 1991); *Whitlock v. Donovan,* 598 F.Supp. 126 (D.D.C. 1984), *aff'd without op.,* 790 F.2d 964 (D.C. Cir. 1986); *Wallace v. Veterans Administration,* 683 F.Supp. 758 (D.Kan. 1988)); dyslexia (*Stutts v. Freeman,* 694 F.2d 666 (11th Cir. 1983)); manic-depressive disorders (including severe depression) (*Overton v. Reilly,* 977 F.2d 1190 (7th Cir. 1992); *Gardner v. Morris,* 752 F.2d 1271 (8th Cir. 1985); *Matzo v. Postmaster General,* 685 F.Supp. 260 (D.D.C. 1987), *aff'd without op.,* 861 F.2d 1290 (D.C. Cir. 1988); *Carty v. Carlin,* 623 F.Supp. 1181 (D.Md. 1985); *Guice-Mills v. Derwinski,* 772 F.Supp. 188 (S.D.N.Y. 1991), *aff'd,* 967 F.2d 794 (2d Cir. 1992)); nervous breakdowns and history of psychological treatment (*Doe V. Syracuse School Dist.,* 508 F.Supp. 333 (N.D.N.Y. 1981)); paranoid schizophrenia (*Franklin v. U.S. Postal Service,* 687 F.Supp. 1214 (S.D. Ohio 1988); *Hubbard v. U.S. Postal Service,* 42 F.E.P. Cases (BNA) 1882 (D.Md. 1986)); post-traumatic stress disorders (*Schmidt v. Bell,* 33 F.E.P. Cases (BNA) 839 (E.D. Pa. 1983)); severe anxiety disorders (*Shea v. Tisch,* 870 F.2d 786 (1st Cir. 1989); *Pesterfield v. Tennessee Valley Authority,* 941 F.2d 437 (6th Cir. 1991)).

8

Case Law Pertinent to ADA

John H. Feldmann III and Maria C. Brandt

Doe v. Region 13 Mental Health-Mental Retardation Commission, 704 F.2d 1402 (5th Cir. 1983)

A mental health care worker who experienced anxiety, insomnia, and depressive neurosis and exhibited suicidal tendencies was held to be handicapped under the Rehabilitation Act. The court found that her employer was reasonably justified in determining that the health care worker was not "otherwise qualified" for her job and that her dismissal was lawful. She was found not to be otherwise qualified because her suicide or attempted suicide could have a detrimental effect on her patients, and she might influence her patients to accept suicide as a valid option.

Gallagher v. Catto, 778 F.Supp. 570 (D.D.C. 1991)

The court held that an employee's alcoholism was a handicapping condition under the Rehabilitation Act. The employee was rightfully terminated under the Rehabilitation Act, however, when he did not adhere to his "firm choice agreement" of treatment or discipline with his employer. The court held that the employer had reasonably accommodated the employee by allowing him leaves of absence and reassignment but that further accommodation would constitute undue hardship because of the employee's disruptive behavior and his inability to work efficiently.

Whitlock v. Donovan, 598 F.Supp. 126 (D.D.C. 1984),
aff'd without op., 790 F.2d 964 (D.C. Cir. 1986)

The employer improperly discharged an alcoholic employee under the Rehabilitation Act where it did not provide reasonable accommodation. A reasonable accommodation which should have been offered was a "firm choice agreement" of reentering the appropriate treatment program or facing suspension or other disciplinary action. In addition, leave without pay could be another reasonable accommodation. The court held that reinstatement was not the proper remedy. Rather, the employee should be allowed to reapply for a job.

Wallace v. Veterans Administration, 683 F.Supp. 758
(D.Kan. 1988)

A drug addiction was found to be a handicap under the Rehabilitation Act. The employer's refusal to hire a recovering drug addict because of her addiction was not lawful where the employer, a hospital, could have reasonably accommodated the nurse by allowing another registered nurse to administer narcotics when necessary, and this accommodation would not jeopardize the functioning of the hospital. The plaintiff was awarded back pay, back benefits, attorney's fees, and the next available registered nurse position at the hospital.

Stutts v. Freeman, 694 F.2d 666 (11th Cir. 1983)

The employer violated the Rehabilitation Act by basing an employment decision relating to a dyslexic employee on a written rather than an oral test. The court determined that the employer had not made an appropriate reasonable accommodation.

Overton v. Reilly, 977 F.2d 1190 (7th Cir. 1992)

A severely depressed employee was found to be covered by the Rehabilitation Act. The court held that a summary judgment in favor of the employer who discharged the employee was not proper because there were genuine issues of material fact as to whether the employee was otherwise qualified for the job and whether the employer failed to provide any reasonable accommodations.

Gardner v. Morris, 752 F.2d 1271 (8th Cir. 1985)

The employer was allowed to refuse to transfer a manic-depressive employee who took lithium carbonate to a remote location out of the United States. All possible accommodations involving monitoring of the lithium treatment was unduly burdensome to the employer because of the lack of adequate medical facilities at the new site and the prohibitive cost of making facilities available to the employee.

Matzo v. Postmaster General, 685 F.Supp. 260 (D.D.C. 1987), *aff'd without op.,* 861 F.2d 1290 (D.C. Cir. 1988)

A secretary who had a manic-depressive illness was properly dismissed as not otherwise qualified for her job where she exhibited erratic and disruptive behavior at work and extensive absenteeism. Her employer had reasonably accommodated her by hiring a temporary worker while she was absent and offered to rehire her at a lower grade (with, presumably, less stressful job requirements).

Carty v. Carlin, 623 F.Supp. 1181 (D.Md. 1985)

The court held on summary judgment that an employee with an anxiety condition and manic-depression (along with some physical disabilities) was properly discharged rather than transferred where the employee was found not to be a "qualified handicapped person" under the law. The employee was not "otherwise qualified" because he could not perform the essential functions of his job under any circumstances. In addition, the court held that the duty of an employer to accommodate does not require an employer to reassign a handicapped person as a reasonable accommodation.

Guice-Mills v. Derwinski, 772 F.Supp. 188 (S.D.N.Y. 1991), aff'd, 967 F.2d 794 (2d Cir. 1992)

Plaintiff was found to be handicapped where she experienced severe depression and anxiety. Plaintiff was held not to be "otherwise qualified" because she was unable to meet the job requirements of the job she held. The employer correctly offered her the reasonable accommodation of a different job assignment, which the plaintiff refused. Plaintiff's requested change in her working hours was held not a possible reasonable accommodation because it would have caused the employer unreasonable administrative burden.

Doe v. Syracuse School Dist., 508 F.Supp. 333 (N.D.N.Y. 1981)

The court awarded summary judgment in favor of a job applicant under the Rehabilitation Act where the employer made a pre-employment inquiry as to the mental health of a prospective employee. The pre-employment questionaire asked whether the prospective employee had ever experienced a nervous breakdown or had psychiatric treatment. The rejected applicant who disclosed a prior nervous breakdown was awarded damages and an injunction.

Franklin v. U.S. Postal Service, 687 F.Supp. 1214 (S.D. Ohio 1988)

Plaintiff who suffered from paranoid schizophrenia was covered by the Rehabilitation Act but was not an "otherwise qualified" individual because she failed to take medication consistently. The employer's attempts at reasonable accommodation by allowing the employee prolonged leaves of absence without pay were found to be adequate.

Hubbard v. U.S. Postal Service, 42 F.E.P. Cases (BNA) 1882 (D.Md. 1986)

The court granted a summary judgment in favor of the employer where the former employee did not tell his employer of his paranoid schizophrenia until after he had been discharged. The court held that the employee failed to state a claim under the Rehabilitation Act because he failed to show that the employer was aware of the handicap and therefore could not have known to provide a reasonable accommodation.

Schmidt v. Bell, 33 F.E.P. Cases (BNA) 839 (E.D. Pa. 1983)

Plaintiff, who experienced Vietnam Veterans' Syndrome, a delayed post-traumatic stress disorder, was held not to be otherwise qualified for his job. The court held that his discharge was proper because he could not effectively function in his current job, and that reassignment would not be a reasonable accommodation since the reassignment would not insulate him from legitimate criticism, which caused his disorder to begin to operate.

Shea v. Tisch, 870 F.2d 786 (1st Cir. 1989)

The court upheld a summary judgment in favor of the employer where the employee, who suffered from an anxiety disorder, was reasonably accommodated but a reasonable accommodation did not include a reassignment as requested by the employee. Reassignment was not possible because to do so would violate the rights of other employees under the collective bargaining agreement.

Pesterfield v. Tennessee Valley Authority, 941 F.2d 437
(6th Cir. 1991)

The court held that an employer properly exercised its objective good faith belief that an employee who suffered from anxiety was not fit to return to work and thus not an "otherwise qualified" employee under the Rehabilitation Act. The employer was also correct in determining that the employee could not return to work safely under any accommodation the employer could provide.

Appendix 1

*World Health Organization
International Classification
of Impairments, Disabilities,
and Handicaps (ICIDH)*

IMPAIRMENT

Definition   In the context of health experience, an impairment is
any loss or abnormality of psychological, physiological,
or anatomical structure or function

(Note : "Impairment" is more inclusive than "disorder"
in that it covers losses – e.g., the loss of a leg is an
impairment, but not a disorder)

Characteristics   Impairment is characterized by losses or abnormalities
that may be temporary or permanent, and that include
the existence or occurrence of an anomaly, defect, or
loss in a limb, organ, tissue, or other structure of the
body, including the systems of mental function. Impairment represents exteriorization of a pathological
state, and in principle it reflects disturbances at the
level of the organ

LIST OF TWO-DIGIT CATEGORIES OF IMPAIRMENT

1   INTELLECTUAL IMPAIRMENTS

Impairments of intelligence (10-14)
10   Profound mental retardation
11   Severe mental retardation
12   Moderate mental retardation
13   Other mental retardation
14   Other impairment of intelligence

Impairments of memory (15-16)
15   Amnesia
16   Other impairment of memory

Impairments of thinking (17-18)
17   Impairment of flow and form of thought processes
18   Impairment of thought content

Other intellectual impairments (19)
19   Other intellectual impairment

2   OTHER PSYCHOLOGICAL IMPAIRMENTS

Impairments of consciousness and wakefulness (20-22)
20   Impairment of clarity of consciousness and of the quality of conscious experience
21   Intermittent impairment of consciousness
22   Other impairment of consciousness and wakefulness

Impairments of perception and attention (23-24)
23   Impairment of perception
24   Impairment of attention

Impairments of emotive and volitional functions (25-28)

25   Impairment of drives

26   Impairment of emotion, affect, and mood

27   Impairment of volition

28   Impairment of psychomotor functions

Behaviour pattern impairments (29)

29   Impairment of behaviour pattern

3   LANGUAGE IMPAIRMENTS

Impairments of language functions (30-34)

30   Severe impairment of communication

31   Impairment of language comprehension and use

32   Impairment of extralinguistic and sublinguistic functions

33   Impairment of other linguistic functions

34   Other impairment of learning

Impairments of speech (35-39)

35   Impairment of voice production

36   Other impairment of voice function

37   Impairment of speech form

38   Impairment of speech content

39   Other impairment of speech

4   AURAL IMPAIRMENTS

Impairments of auditory sensitivity (40-45)

40   Total or profound impairment of development of hearing

41   Profound bilateral hearing loss

42   Profound hearing impairment in one ear with moderately severe impairment of the other ear

43   Moderately severe bilateral hearing impairment

44   Profound hearing impairment in one ear with moderate or lesser impairment of the other ear

45   Other impairment of auditory sensitivity

Other auditory and aural impairments (46-49)

46   Impairment of speech discrimination
47   Other impairment of auditory function
48   Impairment of vestibular and balance function
49   Other impairment of aural function

5   OCULAR IMPAIRMENTS

Impairments of visual acuity (50-55)

50   Absence of eye
51   Profound visual impairment of both eyes
52   Profound visual impairment of one eye with low vision in the other
     eye
53   Moderate visual impairment of both eyes
54   Profound visual impairment of one eye
55   Other impairment of visual acuity

Other visual and ocular impairments (56-58)

56   Visual field impairment
57   Other visual impairment
58   Other ocular impairment

6   VISCERAL IMPAIRMENTS

Impairments of internal organs (60-66)

60   Mechanical and motor impairment of internal organs
61   Impairment of cardiorespiratory function
62   Impairment of gastrointestinal function
63   Impairment of urinary function
64   Impairment of reproductive function
65   Deficiency of internal organs
66   Other impairment of internal organs

Impairments of other special functions (67-69)

67   Impairment of sexual organs
68   Impairment of mastication and swallowing
69   Impairment related to olfaction and other special functions

7   SKELETAL IMPAIRMENTS

Impairments of head and trunk regions (70)

70   Impairment of head and trunk regions

Mechanical and motor impairments of limbs (71-74)

71   Mechanical impairment of limb
72   Spastic paralysis of more than one limb
73   Other paralysis of limb
74   Other motor impairment of limb

Deficiencies of limbs (75-79)

75   Transverse deficiency of proximal parts of limb
76   Transverse deficiency of distal parts of limb
77   Longitudinal deficiency of proximal parts of upper limb
78   Longitudinal deficiency of proximal parts of lower limb
79   Longitudinal deficiency of distal parts of limb

8   DISFIGURING IMPAIRMENTS

Disfigurements of head and trunk regions (80-83)

80   Deficiency in head region
81   Structural deformity in head and trunk regions
82   Other disfigurement of head
83   Other disfigurement of trunk

Disfigurements of limbs (84-87)

84 Failure of differentiation of parts
85 Other congenital malformation
86 Other structural disfigurement
87 Other disfigurement

Other disfiguring impairments (88-89)

88 Abnormal orifice
89 Other disfiguring impairment

9 GENERALIZED, SENSORY, AND OTHER IMPAIRMENTS

Generalized impairments (90-94)

90 Multiple impairment
91 Severe impairment of continence
92 Undue susceptibility to trauma
93 Metabolic impairment
94 Other generalized impairment

Sensory impairments (95-98)

95 Sensory impairment of head
96 Sensory impairment of trunk
97 Sensory impairment of upper limb
98 Other sensory impairment

Other impairments (99)

99 Other impairment

1   INTELLECTUAL IMPAIRMENTS

Intellectual impairments include those of intelligence, memory, and thought
Excludes : impairments of language and learning (30-34)

IMPAIRMENTS OF INTELLIGENCE (10-14)

Includes : disturbances of the rate and degree of development of
cognitive functions, such as perception, attention,
memory, and thinking, and their deterioration as a
result of pathological processes

10   Profound mental retardation
IQ under 20
Individuals who may respond to skill training in the use of legs, hands,
and jaws

11   Severe mental retardation
IQ 20-34
Individuals who can profit from systematic habit training

12   Moderate mental retardation
IQ 35-49
Individuals who can learn simple communication, elementary health
and safety habits, and simple manual skills, but do not progress in
functional reading or arithmetic

13   Other mental retardation

13.0   *Mild mental retardation*
IQ 50-70
Individuals who can acquire practical skills and functional reading and
arithmetic abilities with special education, and who can be guided towards social conformity

13.8   *Other*

13.9   *Unspecified*

14   Other impairment of intelligence

14.0   *Global dementia*
Dementia affecting all cognitive functions and skills
Includes : deterioration of cognitive functioning as a result of cerebral
disease or trauma

14.1   *Lacunar or patchy dementia*
With partial preservation of some cognitive functions and skills

14.2   *Other and unspecified dementia*
14.3   *Loss of learned skills*
14.8   *Other*
14.9   *Unspecified*

IMPAIRMENTS OF MEMORY (15-16)

15   Amnesia
        Includes : partial or complete loss of memory for past events, and
                        inability to register, retain, or retrieve new information
15.0   *Retrograde amnesia*
        Impaired memory for happenings prior to some well-identified event
15.1   *Impairment of long-term memory*
15.2   *Impairment of recent memory*
        Includes : congrade amnesia, impaired ability to acquire new infor-
                        mation
15.3   *Psychogenic amnesia*
        Irregularity of pattern of memory loss
15.4   *Impairment of memory for shapes*
15.5   *Impairment of memory for words*
15.6   *Impairment of memory for figures*
15.8   *Other*
15.9   *Unspecified*

16   Other impairment of memory

        Memory includes the capacity to register, retain, and reproduce infor-
        mation
        Includes : false memories and distortions of memory content
16.0   *Confabulation*
16.1   *Memory illusions*
        Paramnesia
16.2   *Cryptomnesia*
        Recall of facts or events without recognizing them as memories
16.3   *Other distortion of memory content*
16.4   *Forgetfulness*
16.8   *Other*
16.9   *Unspecified*

IMPAIRMENTS OF THINKING (17-18)

17   Impairment of flow and form of thought processes
Includes : disturbances affecting the speed and organization of thought processes, and the ability to form logical sequences of ideas

17.0   *Impairment of conceptualization or abstraction*
Relates to the ability to interpret the meaning of what is perceived, to integrate perceptions, to form meaningful relations among perceptions, and to abstract

17.1   *Impairment of logical thinking*
Relates to the ability to relate ideas hierarchically

17.2   *Slowness of thought*

17.3   *Acceleration of thought*

17.4   *Perseveration*
Includes : "getting stuck", repeating phrases, and constantly returning to same topic

17.5   *Circumstantial thinking*

17.6   *Obsessional ideas*

17.7   *Flight of ideas*
Includes : association of words by sound or rhyme

17.8   *Other*
Includes : incoherence of thought processes

17.9   *Unspecified*

18   Impairment of thought content
Includes : restriction of thought content, excessive or unrealistic emphasis on and preoccupation with a particular set of ideas to the exclusion of critical examination of the ideas, and false beliefs not amenable to correction through logical argument and reality testing

18.0   *Poverty of thought content*

18.1   *Overvalued ideas*

18.2   *Paranoid delusions*
A delusion is a false belief, impervious to the force of reason, and not shared by others of similar education and cultural background. A paranoid delusion or idea of reference is a delusion in which the individual considers that things in his surroundings are happening especially in connexion with him

18.3   *Depressive delusions*
         Includes : delusions of guilt and impoverishment
18.4   *Delusional jealousy*
18.5   *Delusions of grandeur*
18.6   *Fantastic delusions*
18.7   *Hypochondriacal and nihilistic delusions*
18.8   *Other delusions*
18.9   *Other and unspecified*

OTHER INTELLECTUAL IMPAIRMENTS (19)

19   Other intellectual impairment

         Includes : Impairments of gnosis and praxis functions, where there is
                    disturbance of higher cortical functions underlying the
                    recognition and purposeful manipulation of objects
19.0   *Agnosia*
         Disturbed ability to recognise objects in the absence of impairments
         of consciousness, memory, and thinking
19.1   *Apraxia*
         Disturbed ability to perform learned purposeful movements in the
         absence of impairments of consciousness, memory, thinking, and
         motor capacity
19.2   *Acalculia*
         Disturbed ability to count and operate with numbers in the absence
         of impairments of consciousness, memory, and thinking
19.3   *Impairment of openness to new ideas*
19.4   *Misinterpretation*
         A misinterpretation is a false construction put by the individual on
         an occurrence
19.8   *Other*
19.9   *Unspecified*

2   OTHER PSYCHOLOGICAL IMPAIRMENTS

Psychological impairments have been interpreted so as to include interference with the basic functions constituting mental life. For the purposes of this scheme, the functions listed as being impaired are those that normally indicate the presence of basic neurophysiological and psychological mechanisms. The level of organization of these functions is that usually recorded in a clinical examination of the central nervous system and in the examination of "mental status". In addition, some more complex psychological functions to do with drives, emotional control, and reality testing have also been included.

Conventionally symptoms such as hallucinations and delusions are usually thought of as very closely related to what have been defined here as impairments. In terms of the classification they can be regarded as the result of impairment of some essential psychological processes, which must normally exist even though we are as yet largely ignorant of their nature. For instance, severe anxiety symptoms can be thought of as an impairment of autonomic response control mechanisms; the same applies to morbid depressive affect, and to hypomanic affect. Similarly, hallucinations presumably result from impairment of mechanisms differentiating between self and non-self, while delusions indicate impairment of analogous mechanisms concerned with reality testing. For the purposes of the classification, symptoms have been included among impairments with the understanding that there is an inferred impairment of some underlying complex psychological mechanism.

Interferences with behaviour that represent complex purposeful and integrated sequences of interaction with and response to the environment and other persons are, for this purpose, properly regarded as disabilities rather than impairments.

IMPAIRMENTS OF CONSCIOUSNESS AND WAKEFULNESS (20-22)

20   **Impairment of clarity of consciousness and the quality of conscious experience**

Includes : various degrees of diminished wakefulness, and states characterized by changes in the level of wakefulness combined with altered awareness of self and the surrounding world

Excludes : Intermittent impairment of consciousness (21)

20.0   *Unconsciousness*
        Includes : coma, sopor, and stupor
20.1   *Clouding of consciousness*
        Includes : transitional syndrome or post-concussional state
20.2   *Narrowing of field of consciousness*
        Includes : when due to affect
20.3   *Delirium*
        Includes : twilight states
20.4   *Other confusional state*
        Includes : disorientation for time, place, and persons
20.5   *Dissociative state*
20.6   *Trance-like state*
        Includes : hypnotic state
20.7   *Akinetic mutism*
20.8   *Other*
20.9   *Unspecified*

21   Intermittent impairment of consciousness

Includes : intermittent ictal disturbances characterized by a total or partial loss of consciousness or by states of altered awareness, and a variety of local cerebral signs and symptoms

21.0   *Profound intermittent interruption of consciousness*
        Includes : epilepsy with frequency of seizures of once per day or greater
21.1   *Severe intermittent interruption of consciousness*
        Includes : epilepsy with frequency of seizures of once per week or greater
21.2   *Moderate intermittent interruption of consciousness*
        Includes : epilepsy with frequency of seizures of once per month or greater
21.3   *Mild intermittent interruption of consciousness*
        Includes : epilepsy with frequency of seizures less than once per month
21.4   *Intermittent disturbance of consciousness*
        Includes : psychomotor epilepsy
21.5   *Other seizures*
        Includes : petit mal
21.6   *Other intermittent interruption of consciousness*
        Includes : syncope and drop-attacks
21.7   *Fugue states*

21.8   *Other*
21.9   *Unspecified*

22   Other impairment of consciousness and wakefulness
Includes : impairments of the sleep/wakefulness cycle, both disturb-
            ances affecting the quantity, quality, and pattern of the
            processes of sleep and wakefulness, and impairments of
            autonomic control of bodily functions that are influenced
            by the sleep cycle

22.0   *Difficulty in getting off to sleep*
22.1   *Premature awakening from sleep*
        Includes : insomnia NOS
22.2   *Hypersomnia*
        Excessive sleeping
22.3   *Other impairment of sleep/wakefulness pattern*
        Includes : narcolepsy
22.4   *Enuresis nocturna*
22.5   *Other abnormality of acitivity during sleep*
        Includes : sleep-walking and sleep-talking
22.6   *Other impairm ent of sleep/wakefulness cycle*
22.7   *Sleepiness*
        Includes : somnolence
22.8   *Other*
        Includes : impairment of awareness (which is an undifferentiated
                    response to stimulus)
22.9   *Unspecified*

IMPAIRMENTS OF PERCEPTION AND ATTENTION (23-24)

Includes : disturbances of the functions enabling an individual to
            receive through the senses, to process information about
            the individual's own body and his environment, and to
            focus selectively on aspects or parts of such information

23   Impairment of perception

23.0   *Impairment of the intensity of perception*
        Includes : changes in the degree to which qualities and attributes of
                    objects are perceived as vivid and impressing on the mind
        23.00   Uniform dulling of perception

23.01	Selective dulling of perception Includes : dulling in specific modalities
23.02	Uniform heightening of perception
23.03	Selective heightening of perception Includes : hypersensitivity to noise
23.08	Other
23.09	Unspecified

23.1 *Distortion of perception*
Includes : illusions,disturbed percepts where the objective content of sense data received in different modalities is distorted — something actually to be seen or heard is experienced as something else
Excludes : depersonalization (23.30)

23.10	Optical illusions
23.11	Acoustic illusions
23.12	Tactile illusions
23.13	Kinaesthetic illusions
23.14	Illusions in other sense modalities
23.15	Composite illusions Includes : pareidolic imagery
23.18	Other
23.19	Unspecified

23.2 *False perception*
Includes : hallucinations and pseudohallucinations, false or abnormal percepts that are not based on objective sense data

23.20	Visual hallucinations
23.21	Auditory hallucinations
23.22	Tactile hallucinations
23.23	Olfactory hallucinations
23.24	Gustatory hallucinations
23.25	Other hallucinations
23.26	Pseudohallucinations Includes : those in any sense modality
23.27	Oneroid or dream-like hallucinatory state
23.28	Other
23.29	Unspecified

23.3 *Disturbance of body awareness*

23.30   Depersonalization

Experiences of alienation from one's own body, and the experience that one's relationship to the environment and surroundings (and vice versa) is altered

23.31   Derealization

Alteration of the feeling of reality/unreality and familiarity/unfamiliarity accompanying the perception of objects

Includes : déjà vu, jamais vu, and déjà vécu experiences

23.32   Body image disorder

Includes : phantom limb experiences

23.38   Other

23.39   Unspecified

23.4   *Disturbances of time and space perception*

Includes : time-standing-still, micropsy, and macropsy experiences

23.5   *Impairment of reality testing*

Includes : loss of ability to distinguish fantasy from reality

23.8   *Other*

23.9   *Unspecified*

24   Impairment of attention

Includes : disturbances of the intensity, span, and mobility of attention, the latter being a differentiated response to specific stimulus

24.0   *Distractibility*

24.1   *Impaired concentration*

24.2   *Narrowing of attention span*

24.3   *Impaired ability to shift focus of attention*

Includes : fixed attention

24.4   *Blank spells*

Includes : sudden stoppage or inattention while speaking for a few seconds or longer (may be due to thought-blocking or hallucination)

24.5   *Inattentiveness*

24.6   *Impairment of alertness*

Includes : diminished ability to stay alert as reflected by facial expression, speech, or posture

24.8   *Other*

24.9   *Unspecified*

IMPAIRMENTS OF EMOTIVE AND VOLITIONAL FUNCTIONS (25-28)

Refer to functions which contribute predispositions to action and purposeful behaviour

25   Impairment of drives

Includes : increase, decrease, or changes of pattern of various behaviours related to basic physiological needs or instincts

Excludes : impairment of volition (27)

25.0   *Decreased appetite*

Includes : anorexia

25.1   *Increased appetite*

Includes : hyperorexia and bulimia

25.2   *Impairment of heterosexual role*

Includes : homosexuality and lack of interest in a relationship or contact with individuals of the opposite sex

25.3   *Decrease of libido*

Includes : loss of libido

25.4   *Other impairment of sexual performance*

In the presence of normal libido

Includes : other disturbances of sexual functioning

Excludes : impairment of reproductive function (64) and of sexual organs (67)

25.40   Impotence

25.41   Ejaculatio praecox

25.42   Frigidity

25.48   Other

25.49   Unspecified

25.5   *Alcohol dependence*

Includes : alcoholism

25.6   *Other drug dependence*

Includes : drug addiction

25.7   *Other pathological craving*

Includes : states of pathological craving related to substance dependence, and alcohol abuse

25.8	*Other*	
	25.80	Inability to sustain goals
	25.81	Impairment of motivation
	25.88	Other
25.9	*Unspecified*	

26   **Impairment of emotion, affect, and mood**

Includes : disturbances of the intensity and quality of feelings and their somatic accompaniments, and disturbances of the duration and stability of feeling states

Excludes : pathological affect leading to narrowing of field of consciousness (20.3)

26.0   *Anxiety*

Includes : tense, worried look or posture, fearful apprehensive look, frightened tone of voice, and tremor

Excludes : tremor NOS (74.90)

26.00   Pathological anxiety

Includes : free-floating anxiety

26.01   Phobic anxiety

Includes : panic attacks

26.08   Other

26.09   Unspecified

26.1   *Depression*

Includes : anhedonia, and features such as sad, mournful look, tears, gloomy tone of voice, deep sighing, and choking of voice on depressing topic

26.2   *Other blunting of affect*

Includes : apathy, expressionless face or voice, uniform blunting whatever the topic of conversation, indifference to distressing topics, and flatness of affect

26.3   *Gross excitement*

Includes : the individual is manic, or throws things, runs or jumps around, waves arms wildly, shouts, or screams

26.4   *Other excitement*

Includes : euphoria, elation, hypomania, and unduly cheerful or smiling.

Excludes : psychomotor excitement (28.2)

26.5   *Irritability*
        Includes :   angry outbursts
26.6   *Emotional lability*
        Includes : lability of one mood, changing from one mood to
                     another, and proneness to periods of depression or
                     elation
26.7   *Incongruity of affect*
        Includes : emotion shown but not congruent with topic, and
                     ambivalent affect

26.8   *Other*
        26.80   "Catastrophic reaction"
        26.81   Attempted control of affect display
                     Includes : attempt to suppress crying or anger, or to
                           fake a socially appropriate affect

        26.82   Restlessness
        26.83   Feelings of guilt
        26.84   Emotional immaturity
        26.85   Distress NEC
        26.88   Other

26.9   *Unspecified*
        Includes : emotionally disturbed NOS, emotional impairment NEC

27   **Impairment of volition**
        Includes : disturbances of the capacity for purposeful behaviour
                     and control of own actions

        Excludes : obsessional traits (29.5) and mutism (30.0)

27.0   *Lack of initiative*
        Includes : impairment of manifestations of independent or un-
                     prompted action and self determination (the latter
                     including expression of personal opinion such as
                     spontaneous criticism or disagreement (not nega-
                     tivism, 27.3), situation-relevant acts such as closing
                     a door or lifting an object from the floor, asking
                     questions, and making requests or demands)

27.1   *Restriction of interests*
        Includes : loss of interests
27.2   *Overcompliance*
        Includes : excessive cooperation with elements of passivity,
                     and automatic submission

27.3   *Negativism*

27.4   *Ambitendence*

27.5   *Compulsions*
        Includes : rituals

27.6   *Impairment of impulse control*
        Includes : impulsive acts

27.8   *Other*
        Includes : impairment of adaptability, and other impairment
                   of cooperation (e.g., misleading responses such as
                   consistently negative responses and frequent self-
                   contradiction, or appearance of being deliberately
                   misleading)
        Excludes : Fatigability (28.5)

27.9   *Unspecified*

28   **Impairment of psychomotor functions**
        Includes : disturbances in the speed, rate, and quality of voluntary
                   movements in the presence of an intact neural motor
                   apparatus
        Excludes : involuntary movements of face (70.21), head (70.31),
                   and body (70.54), and facial mannerisms (70.22)

28.0   *Slowness*
        Includes : slowness of psychic tempo, reduction of rate or speed
                   of voluntary movements, and delays in responding to
                   questions or in initiating requested tasks or movements
                   (such as walking abnormally slowly, delay in perform-
                   ing movements, slowness of speech with long pauses
                   before answering or between words, and reduction of
                   facial movements)
        Excludes : indistinct speech (35.5)

28.1   *Other underactivity*
        Includes : hypoactivity, semistuporous states, and reduction of
                   extent of voluntary movements (such as sitting abnor-
                   mally still, near total lack of voluntary movement,
                   "doing nothing", and immobility of face)
        Excludes : stupor (20.0)

28.2   *Psychomotor excitement*

28.3   *Hyperkinesia in children*

28.4   *Other overactivity*
        Includes : over-talkativeness, pacing up and down restlessly, and
                   not sitting down for a minute

28.5   *Fatigability*
       Fatigue out of proportion to demands experienced
       Includes : abnormal fall-off in alertness or speed of response or
                  initiative
       Excludes : sleepiness (22.7) and generalized fatigue (94.6)
28.8   *Other*
28.9   *Unspecified*

BEHAVIOUR PATTERN IMPAIRMENTS (29)

Refer to habitual patterns of behaviour that may interfere with social
adjustment and functioning. Such patterns of behaviour may be
present since adolescence and throughout most of adult life (e.g., in
personality disorders), or may occur as persisting sequelae of neuro-
logical or mental illnesses. They manifest themselves mainly as
accentuated character traits

Excludes : mood instability (26.6)

29   Impairment of behaviour pattern
29.0   *Suspiciousness*
29.1   *Social withdrawal*
       Includes : active avoidance of verbal or non-verbal interaction with
                  other people, or of being in the physical presence of other
                  people (e.g., avoidance of customarily expected social
                  activities outside the home such as visiting kin or friends,
                  going out with friends, and participating in games)

29.2   *Excessive shyness*
       Includes : excessive sensitivity and vulnerability, and other impair-
                  ment of ability to mix with people
29.3   *Hypochondriasis*
29.4   *Worrying*
       Excludes : anxiety (26.0)
29.5   *Obsessional traits*
       Includes : insecurity, indecisiveness, and repetition compulsion
29.6   *Other phobias*
       Includes : agoraphobia
29.7   *Hostility*
       Includes : aggressivity, being uncooperative, angry, overtly hostile.
                  discontented, antagonistic, threatening, or violent
                  (hitting out at or attacking others)

29.8	*Other*	
	29.80	Histrionic traits
	29.81	Perplexity
		Includes : puzzlement
	29.82	Self-injury
		Includes : head banging, picking at sores, and beating eyes
	29.83	Other destructiveness
		Includes : damaging furniture and tearing up pages, maga- zines, or clothing
	29.84	Attention-seeking
		Includes : will not leave (other) adults
	29.85	Solitary behaviour
	29.88	Other
29.9	*Unspecified*	
		Includes : personality disorder NEC

DISABILITY

Definition   In the context of health experience, a disability is any
                      restriction or lack (resulting from an impairment) of
                      ability to perform an activity in the manner or within
                      the range considered normal for a human being

Characteristics   Disability is characterized by excesses or deficiencies
                      of customarily expected activity performance and
                      behaviour, and these may be temporary or permanent,
                      reversible or irreversible, and progressive or regressive.
                      Disabilities may arise as a direct consequence of impair-
                      ment or as a response by the individual, particularly
                      psychologically, to a physical, sensory, or other impair-
                      ment.   Disability represents objectification of an
                      impairment, and as such it reflects disturbances at the
                      level of the person

                      Disability is concerned with abilities, in the form of
                      composite activities and behaviours, that are generally
                      accepted as essential components of everyday life.
                      Examples include disturbances in behaving in an
                      appropriate manner, in personal care (such as excretory
                      control and the ability to wash and feed oneself), in the
                      performance of other activities of daily living, and in
                      locomotor activities (such as the ability to walk)

LIST OF TWO-DIGIT CATEGORIES OF DISABILITY

1   BEHAVIOUR DISABILITIES

Awareness disabilities (10-16)

10   Self-awareness disability
11   Disability relating to location in time and space
12   Other identification disability
13   Personal safety disability
14   Disability relating to situational behaviour
15   Knowledge acquisition disability
16   Other educational disability

Disabilities in relations (17-19)

17   Family role disability
18   Occupational role disability
19   Other behaviour disability

2   COMMUNICATION DISABILITIES

Speaking disabilities (20-22)

20   Disability in understanding speech
21   Disability in talking
22   Other speaking disability

Listening disabilities (23-24)

23   Disability in listening to speech
24   Other listening disability

Seeing disabilities (25-27)

25   Disability in gross visual tasks
26   Disability in detailed visual tasks
27   Other disability in seeing and related activities

Other communication disabilities (28-29)

28   Disability in writing
29   Other communication disability

3   PERSONAL CARE DISABILITIES

Excretion disabilities (30-32)

30   Controlled excretory difficulty
31   Uncontrolled excretory difficulty
32   Other excretion disability

Personal hygiene disabilities (33-34)

33   Bathing disability
34   Other personal hygiene disability

Dressing disabilities (35-36)

35   Clothing disability
36   Other dressing disability

Feeding and other personal care disabilities (37-39)

37   Disability in preliminaries to feeding
38   Other feeding disability
39   Other personal care disability

4   LOCOMOTOR DISABILITIES

Ambulation disabilities (40-45)

40   Walking disability
41   Traversing disability
42   Climbing stairs disability
43   Other climbing disability
44   Running disability
45   Other ambulation disability

Confining disabilities (46-47)

46   Transfer disability
47   Transport disability

Other locomotor disabilities (48-49)

48   Lifting disability
49   Other locomotor disability

5   BODY DISPOSITION DISABILITIES

Domestic disability (50-51)

50   Subsistence disability
51   Household disability

Body movement disabilities (52-27)

52   Retrieval disability
53   Reaching disability
54   Other disability in arm function
55   Kneeling disability
56   Crouching disability
57   Other body movement disability

Other body disposition disabilities (58-59)

58   Postural disability
59   Other body disposition disability

6   DEXTERITY DISABILITIES

Daily activity disabilities (60-61)

60   Environmental modulation disability
61   Other daily activity disability

Manual activity disabilities (62-66)

62   Fingering disability
63   Gripping disability
64   Holding disability
65   Handedness disability
66   Other manual activity disability

Other dexterity disabilities (67-69)

67   Foot control disability
68   Other body control disability
69   Other dexterity disability

7   SITUATIONAL DISABILITIES

Dependence and endurance disabilities (70-71)

70   Circumstantial dependence
71   Disability in endurance

Environmental disabilities (72-77)

72   Disability relating to temperature tolerance
73   Disability relating to tolerance of other climatic features
74   Disability relating to tolerance of noise
75   Disability relating to tolerance of illumination
76   Disability relating to tolerance of work stresses
77   Disability relating to tolerance of other environmental factors

Other situational disabilities (78)

78   Other situational disability

8   PARTICULAR SKILL DISABILITIES

9   OTHER ACTIVITY RESTRICTIONS

1   BEHAVIOUR DISABILITIES

Refer to an individual's awareness and ability to conduct himself, both in everyday activities and towards others, and including the ability to learn

Excludes :   communication disabilities (2)

AWARENESS   DISABILITIES   (10 - 16)

Awareness refers to having knowledge

10   Self-awareness disability

Includes :   disturbance of the ability to develop or maintain a mental representation of the identity of the individual's self or body ("body image") and its continuity over time; and disturbance of behaviour resulting from interference with consciousness or sense of identity and confusion (inappropriate interpretation of and response to external events, which expresses itself in agitation, restlessness, and noisiness)

10.0   *Transient self-awareness disability*

10.1   *Disability in body image orientation*

Includes :   disturbance in the mental representation of the individual's body, such as inability in right-left differentiation, "phantom limb" experiences, and other related phenomena

10.2   *Personal uncleanliness*

Includes :   neglect of shaving or state of hair, and dirty clothing

10.3   *Other disturbance of appearance*

Includes :   careless dress or make-up, and appearance that is bizarre (such as "secret documents" and special clothes or ornaments with idiosyncratic meaning, which may be related to delusions), of very inappropriate taste, or conspicuously out of fashion

10.4   *Other disturbance of self-presentation*

Includes :   disturbance of the ability to present a favourable image in social situations, such as by inattention to supportive social routines (e.g., greetings, partings, giving thanks, apologizing, excusing, and reciprocation of these), and lack of "presence" (e.g., total absence of originality, or excessive conformity in demeanour)

Excludes :   intended unconventional behaviour (which is not a disability)

10.8	*Other*
10.9	*Unspecified*

11   Disability relating to location in time and space

Includes :   disturbance of the ability of the individual to correctly
locate external objects, events, and himself in relation
to the dimensions of time and space

11.0	*Transient disability relating to location in time and space*
11.8	*Other*
11.9	*Unspecified*

12   Other identification disability

Includes :   disturbance of the ability to identify objects and persons correctly

12.0   *Transient disability in identifying objects and persons*

12.1   *Conduct out of context*

Conduct that is generally appropriate but which is inappropriate to
the place, time, or stage of maturation

Includes :   cultural shock (such as in immigrants), moving in different identities (e.g., transvestism and passing, such
as black passing for white), pseudo-feeble-mindedness,
and breaking taboos

12.8	*Other*
12.9	*Unspecified*

13   Personal safety disability

Includes :   disturbance of the ability to avoid hazards to the integrity of the individual's body, such as being in hazard
from self-injury or from inability to safeguard self from
danger

13.0   *Liability to self-injury*

Includes :   risk of suicide or self-inflicted injury

13.1   *Personal safety disability in special situations*

Includes :   being in hazard in special situations, such as those related
to travel and transport, occupation, and recreation, including sport

Excludes :   occupational role disability (18)

13.2   *Conduct potentially dangerous to the individual himself*

Includes :   leaving gas taps or fires on

13.3   *Other irresponsible conduct*

Includes :   tossing lighted matches on carpet

13.4   *Getting lost*

13.5   *Other wandering*

Includes :   when inappropriately clad

13.8   *Other*

13.9   *Unspecified*

14   Disability relating to situational behaviour

Includes :   disturbance of the capacity to register and understand relations between objects and persons in situations of daily living

Excludes :   personal safety disability in special situations (13.1)

14.0   *Situation comprehension disability*

Includes :   disturbance of the capacity to perceive, register, or understand relations between things and people

14.1   *Situation interpretation disability*

Includes :   false interpretation of the relations between and meaning of things and people

14.2   *Situation coping disability*

Includes :   disturbance of the ability to perform everyday activities in specific situations, such as outside the home or in the presence of particular animals or other objects

Excludes :   disability in crisis conduct (18.6)

14.8   *Other*

14.9   *Unspecified*

15   Knowledge acquisition disability

Includes :   general disturbance of the ability to learn, such as may arise from impairments of intellect or of the ability to learn new skills

16   Other educational disability

Includes :   other inability to benefit from educational opportunities because of disturbance of specific individual capacities for acquiring, processing, and retaining new information

Excludes :   those arising from communication (2) and other disabilities (3 - 7)

16.9   *Unspecified*
        Includes :   slowing of mental functions NOS

DISABILITIES IN RELATIONS (17 - 19)

17   Family role disability
17.0   *Disability in participation in household activities*
        Includes :   customary common activities such as having meals
                     together, doing domestic chores, going out or visi-
                     ting together, playing games, and watching television,
                     and conduct during these activities, as well as house-
                     hold decision-making, such as decisions about children
                     and money

17.1   *Disability in affective marital role*
        Includes :   affective relationship with steady heterosexual partner
                     or spouse, and communication (such as talking about
                     children, news, and ordinary events), ability to show
                     affection and warmth (but excluding culturally custom-
                     ary outbursts of anger or irritability), and engendering
                     a feeling of being a source of support in the partner

17.2   *Other marital role disability*
        Includes :   disturbance of sexual relations with steady heterosex-
                     ual partner (including occurrence of sexual intercourse
                     and whether both individual and partner find sexual
                     relations satisfactory)

17.3   *Parental role disability*
        Includes :   undertaking and performance of child care tasks appro-
                     priate to the individual's position in household (such as
                     feeding, putting to bed, or taking to school, for small
                     children, and looking after child's needs, for older chil-
                     dren) and taking interest in child (such as playing with,
                     reading to, and taking interest in child's problems or
                     school work)

17.8   *Other family role disability*
17.9   *Unspecified*

18   **Occupational role disability**

Includes :   disturbance of the ability to organize and participate in
routine activities connected with the occupation of time,
not just confined to the performance of work

Excludes :   situational disabilities (70 - 79)

18.0   *Disability in motivation*

Includes :   interference with the ability to work by virtue of
severe impairment of drive

18.1   *Disability in cooperation*

Includes :   inability to cooperate with others and to "give and take"
in social interaction

18.2   *Disability in work routine*

Includes :   other aspects of conformity to work routine (such as
going to work regularly and on time, and observing the
rules)

18.3   *Disability in organizing daily routine*

Includes :   disturbance of the ability to organize activities in tem-
poral sequences, and difficulty in making decisions about
day-to-day matters

18.4   *Other disability in work performance*

Includes :   other inadequacy in performance and output

18.5   *Recreation disability*

Includes :   lack of interest in leisure activities (such as watching
television, listening to radio, reading newspapers or
books, participating in games, and hobbies) and in local
and world events (including efforts to obtain information)

18.6   *Disability in crisis conduct*

Includes :   unsatisfactory or inappropriate responses to incidents
(such as sickness, accident, or other incident affecting
family member or involving other people), emergencies
(such as fire), and other experiences customarily requiring quick decision and action

18.8   *Other occupational role disability*

Includes :   for individuals not working, their interest in obtaining
or returning to work and actual steps undertaken to
this end

Excludes :   other social role disability (19.2)

18.9   *Unspecified*

19   **Other behaviour disability**

Includes :   disturbance of interpersonal relationships outside the household

Excludes :   occupational role disability (18)

19.0   *Antisocial behaviour*

Includes :   severely maladjusted, psychopathic, and delinquent

19.1   *Indifference to accepted social standards*

Includes :   conduct that is embarrassing (such as making sexual suggestions or advances, or lacking restraint in scratching genitals or in passing loud flatus), irreverent (such as singing, making facetious silly jokes or flippant remarks, or being unduly familiar), or histrionic (such as expression of feelings in an exaggerated, dramatic, or histrionic manner)

19.2   *Other social role disability*

Includes :   overt conduct by the individual involving arguments, arrogance, anger, marked irritability, or other friction arising in social situations outside own home (such as with supervisors, co-workers, or customers, if the individual engages in outside work; with neighbours and other people in the community, if the individual has a domestic role; with teachers, administrators, and fellow students, if the individual is a student; and with fellow inhabitants, if the individual lives in communal accommodation)

Excludes :   self-awareness (10) and identification disabilities (11 - 12)

19.3   *Other personality disability*

Includes :   other excess or lack of any customary trait of personality NOS

19.4   *Other severe behaviour disorder*

Includes :   other disturbance of behaviour (such as aggressiveness, destructiveness, extreme overactivity, and attention-seeking) that presents problems in management and that are NEC

19.8   *Other*

19.9   *Unspecified*

Includes : behaviour disorder NOS

Appendix 2

*World Health Organization
International Classification
of Behavioural and Mental
Disorders (ICD-10, 1992)*

List of categories

F00 – F09
Organic, including symptomatic, mental disorders

F00 Dementia in Alzheimer's disease
F00.0 Dementia in Alzheimer's disease with early onset
F00.1 Dementia in Alzheimer's disease with late onset
F00.2 Dementia in Alzheimer's disease, atypical or mixed type
F00.9 Dementia in Alzheimer's disease, unspecified

F01 Vascular dementia
F01.0 Vascular dementia of acute onset
F01.1 Multi-infarct dementia
F01.2 Subcortical vascular dementia
F01.3 Mixed cortical and subcortical vascular dementia
F01.8 Other vascular dementia
F01.9 Vascular dementia, unspecified

F02 Dementia in other diseases classified elsewhere
F02.0 Dementia in Pick's disease
F02.1 Dementia in Creutzfeldt – Jakob disease
F02.2 Dementia in Huntington's disease
F02.3 Dementia in Parkinson's disease
F02.4 Dementia in human immunodeficiency virus [HIV] disease
F02.8 Dementia in other specified diseases classified elsewhere

F03 Unspecified dementia

A fifth character may be added to specify dementia in F00 – F03, as follows:
.x0 Without additional symptoms
.x1 Other symptoms, predominantly delusional
.x2 Other symptoms, predominantly hallucinatory
.x3 Other symptoms, predominantly depressive
.x4 Other mixed symptoms

F04 Organic amnesic syndrome, not induced by alcohol and other psychoactive substances

F05 Delirium, not induced by alcohol and other psychoactive substances
F05.0 Delirium, not superimposed on dementia, so described
F05.1 Delirium, superimposed on dementia
F05.8 Other delirium
F05.9 Delirium, unspecified

F06 Other mental disorders due to brain damage and dysfunction and to physical disease
F06.0 Organic hallucinosis
F06.1 Organic catatonic disorder
F06.2 Organic delusional [schizophrenia-like] disorder
F06.3 Organic mood [affective] disorders
 .30 Oranic manic disorder
 .31 Organic bipolar disorder
 .32 Organic depressive disorder
 .33 Organic mixed affective disorder
F06.4 Organic anxiety disorder
F06.5 Organic dissociative disorder
F06.6 Organic emotionally labile [asthenic] disorder
F06.7 Mild cognitive disorder
F06.8 Other specified mental disorders due to brain damage and dysfunction and to physical disease
F06.9 Unspecified mental disorder due to brain damage and dysfunction and to physical disease

F07 Personality and behavioural disorders due to brain disease, damage and dysfunction
F07.0 Organic personality disorder
F07.1 Postencephalitic syndrome
F07.2 Postconcussional syndrome
F07.8 Other organic personality and behavioural disorders due to brain disease, damage and dysfunction
F07.9 Unspecified organic personality and behavioural disorder due to brain disease, damage and dysfunction

F09 Unspecified organic or symptomatic mental disorder

F10 – F19
Mental and behavioural disorders due to psychoactive substance use

F10. – Mental and behavioural disorders due to use of alcohol

F11. – Mental and behavioural disorders due to use of opioids

F12. – Mental and behavioural disorders due to use of cannabinoids

F13. – Mental and behavioural disorders due to use of sedatives or hypnotics

F14. – Mental and behavioural disorders due to use of cocaine

F15. – Mental and behavioural disorders due to use of other stimulants, including caffeine

F16. – Mental and behavioural disorders due to use of hallucinogens

F17. – Mental and behavioural disorders due to use of tobacco

F18. – Mental and behavioural disorders due to use of volatile solvents

F19. – Mental and behavioural disorders due to multiple drug use and use of other psychoactive substances

Four- and five-character categories may be used to specify the clinical conditions, as follows:

> F1x.0 Acute intoxication
> .00 Uncomplicated
> .01 With trauma or other bodily injury
> .02 With other medical complications
> .03 With delirium
> .04 With perceptual distortions
> .05 With coma
> .06 With convulsions
> .07 Pathological intoxication

F1*x*.1 Harmful use

F1*x*.2 Dependence syndrome
    .20 Currently abstinent
    .21 Currently abstinent, but in a protected environment
    .22 Currently on a clinically supervised maintenance or replacement regime [controlled dependence]
    .23 Currently abstinent, but receiving treatment with aversive or blocking drugs
    .24 Currently using the substance [active dependence]
    .25 Continuous use
    .26 Episodic use [dipsomania]

F1*x*.3 Withdrawal state
    .30 Uncomplicated
    .31 Convulsions

F1*x*.4 Withdrawal state with delirium
    .40 Without convulsions
    .41 With convulsions

F1*x*.5 Psychotic disorder
    .50 Schizophrenia-like
    .51 Predominantly delusional
    .52 Predominantly hallucinatory
    .53 Predominantly polymorphic
    .54 Predominantly depressive symptoms
    .55 Predominantly manic symptoms
    .56 Mixed

F1*x*.6 Amnesic syndrome

F1*x*.7 Residual and late-onset psychotic disorder
    .70 Flashbacks
    .71 Personality or behaviour disorder
    .72 Residual affective disorder
    .73 Dementia
    .74 Other persisting cognitive impairment
    .75 Late-onset psychotic disorder

F1*x*.8 Other mental and behavioural disorders

F1*x*.9 Unspecified mental and behavioural disorder

F20-F29
Schizophrenia, schizotypal and delusional disorders

F20 Schizophrenia
F20.0 Paranoid schizophrenia
F20.1 Hebephrenic schizophrenia
F20.2 Catatonic schizophrenia
F20.3 Undifferentiated schizophrenia
F20.4 Post-schizophrenic depression
F20.5 Residual schizophrenia
F20.6 Simple schizophrenia
F20.8 Other schizophrenia
F20.9 Schizophrenia, unspecified

A fifth character may be used to classify course:

.x0 Continuous
.x1 Episodic with progressive deficit
.x2 Episodic with stable deficit
.x3 Episodic remittent
.x4 Incomplete remission
.x5 Complete remission
.x8 Other
.x9 Period of observation less than one year

F21 Schizotypal disorder

F22 Persistent delusional disorders
F22.0 Delusional disorder
F22.8 Other persistent delusional disorders
F22.9 Persistent delusional disorder, unspecified

F23 Acute and transient psychotic disorders
F23.0 Acute polymorphic psychotic disorder without symptoms of schizophrenia
F23.1 Acute polymorphic psychotic disorder with symptoms of schizophrenia
F23.2 Acute schizophrenia-like psychotic disorder
F23.3 Other acute predominantly delusional psychotic disorders
F23.8 Other acute and transient psychotic disorders
F23.9 Acute and transient psychotic disorders unspecified

A fifth character may be used to identify the presence or absence of associated acute stress:

    .*x*0 Without associated acute stress
    .*x*1 With associated acute stress

F24 Induced delusional disorder

F25 Schizoaffective disorders
F25.0 Schizoaffective disorder, manic type
F25.1 Schizoaffective disorder, depressive type
F25.2 Schizoaffective disorder, mixed type
F25.8 Other schizoaffective disorders
F25.9 Schizoaffective disorder, unspecified

F28 Other nonorganic psychotic disorders

F29 Unspecified nonorganic psychosis

F30 – F39
Mood [affective] disorders

F30 Manic episode
F30.0 Hypomania
F30.1 Mania without psychotic symptoms
F30.2 Mania with psychotic symptoms
F30.8 Other manic episodes
F30.9 Manic episode, unspecified

F31 Bipolar affective disorder
F31.0 Bipolar affective disorder, current episode hypomanic
F31.1 Bipolar affective disorder, current episode manic without psychotic symptoms
F31.2 Bipolar affective disorder, current episode manic with psychotic symptoms
F31.3 Bipolar affective disorder, current episode mild or moderate depression
  .30 Without somatic symptoms
  .31 With somatic symptoms
F31.4 Bipolar affective disorder, current episode severe depression without psychotic symptoms
F31.5 Bipolar affective disorder, current episode severe depression with psychotic symptoms
F31.6 Bipolar affective disorder, current episode mixed
F31.7 Bipolar affective disorder, currently in remission
F31.8 Other bipolar affective disorders
F31.9 Bipolar affective disorder, unspecified

F32 Depressive episode
F32.0 Mild depressive episode
  .00 Without somatic symptoms
  .01 With somatic symptoms
F32.1 Moderate depressive episode
  .10 Without somatic symptoms
  .11 With somatic symptoms
F32.2 Severe depressive episode without psychotic symptoms
F32.3 Severe depressive episode with psychotic symptoms
F32.8 Other depressive episodes
F32.9 Depressive episode, unspecified

F33 Recurrent depressive disorder

F33.0 Recurrent depressive disorder, current episode mild
    .00 Without somatic symptoms
    .01 With somatic symptoms
F33.1 Recurrent depressive disorder, current episode moderate
    .10 Without somatic symptoms
    .11 With somatic symptoms
F33.2 Recurrent depressive disorder, current episode severe without psychotic symptoms
F33.3 Recurrent depressive disorder, current episode severe with psychotic symptoms
F33.4 Recurrent depressive disorder, currently in remission
F33.8 Other recurrent depressive disorders
F33.9 Recurrent depressive disorder, unspecified

F34 Persistent mood [affective] disorders

F34.0 Cyclothymia
F34.1 Dysthymia
F34.8 Other persistent mood [affective] disorders
F34.9 Persistent mood [affective] disorder, unspecified

F38 Other mood [affective] disorders

F38.0 Other single mood [affective] disorders
    .00 Mixed affective episode
F38.1 Other recurrent mood [affective] disorders
    .10 Recurrent brief depressive disorder
F38.8 Other specified mood [affective] disorders

F39 Unspecified mood [affective] disorder

F40 – F48
Neurotic, stress-related and somatoform disorders

F40 Phobic anxiety disorders
F40.0 Agoraphobia
  .00 Without panic disorder
  .01 With panic disorder
F40.1 Social phobias
F40.2 Specific (isolated) phobias
F40.8 Other phobic anxiety disorders
F40.9 Phobic anxiety disorder, unspecified

F41 Other anxiety disorders
F41.0 Panic disorder [episodic paroxysmal anxiety]
F41.1 Generalized anxiety disorder
F41.2 Mixed anxiety and depressive disorder
F41.3 Other mixed anxiety disorders
F41.8 Other specified anxiety disorders
F41.9 Anxiety disorder, unspecified

F42 Obsessive – compulsive disorder
F42.0 Predominantly obsessional thoughts or ruminations
F42.1 Predominantly compulsive acts [obsessional rituals]
F42.2 Mixed obsessional thoughts and acts
F42.8 Other obsessive – compulsive disorders
F42.9 Obsessive – compulsive disorder, unspecified

F43 Reaction to severe stress, and adjustment disorders
F43.0 Acute stress reaction
F43.1 Post-traumatic stress disorder
F43.2 Adjustment disorders
  .20 Brief depressive reaction
  .21 Prolonged depressive reaction
  .22 Mixed anxiety and depressive reaction
  .23 With predominant disturbance of other emotions
  .24 With predominant disturbance of conduct
  .25 With mixed disturbance of emotions and conduct
  .28 With other specified predominant symptoms
F43.8 Other reactions to severe stress
F43.9 Reaction to severe stress, unspecified

F44 Dissociative [conversion] disorders

F44.0 Dissociative amnesia

F44.1 Dissociative fugue

F44.2 Dissociative stupor

F44.3 Trance and possession disorders

F44.4 Dissociative motor disorders

F44.5 Dissociative convulsions

F44.6 Dissociative anaesthesia and sensory loss

F44.7 Mixed dissociative [conversion] disorders

F44.8 Other dissociative [conversion] disorders

    .80 Ganser's syndrome

    .81 Multiple personality disorder

    .82 Transient dissociate [conversion] disorders occurring in childhood and adolescence

    .88 Other specified dissociative [conversion] disorders

F44.9 Dissociative [conversion] disorder, unspecified

F45 Somatoform disorders

F45.0 Somatization disorder

F45.1 Undifferentiated somatoform disorder

F45.2 Hypochondriacal disorder

F45.3 Somatoform autonomic dysfunction

    .30 Heart and cardiovascular system

    .31 Upper gastrointestinal tract

    .32 Lower gastrointestinal tract

    .33 Respiratory system

    .34 Genitourinary system

    .38 Other organ or system

F45.4 Persistent somatoform pain disorder

F45.8 Other somatoform disorders

F45.9 Somatoform disorder, unspecified

F48 Other neurotic disorders

F48.0 Neurasthenia

F48.1 Depersonalization – derealization syndrome

F48.8 Other specified neurotic disorders

F48.9 Neurotic disorder, unspecified

F50 – F59
Behavioural syndromes associated with physiological disturbances and physical factors

F50 Eating disorders
F50.0 Anorexia nervosa
F50.1 Atypical anorexia nervosa
F50.2 Bulimia nervosa
F50.3 Atypical bulimia nervosa
F50.4 Overeating associated with other psychological disturbances
F50.5 Vomiting associated with other psychological disturbances
F50.8 Other eating disorders
F50.9 Eating disorder, unspecified

F51 Nonorganic sleep disorders
F51.0 Nonorganic insomnia
F51.1 Nonorganic hypersomnia
F51.2 Nonorganic disorder of the sleep-wake schedule
F51.3 Sleepwalking [somnambulism]
F51.4 Sleep terrors [night terrors]
F51.5 Nightmares
F51.8 Other nonorganic sleep disorders
F51.9 Nonorganic sleep disorder, unspecified

F52 Sexual dysfunction, not caused by organic disorder or disease
F52.0 Lack or loss of sexual desire
F52.1 Sexual aversion and lack of sexual enjoyment
    .10 Sexual aversion
    .11 Lack of sexual enjoyment
F52.2 Failure of genital response
F52.3 Orgasmic dysfunction
F52.4 Premature ejaculation
F52.5 Nonorganic vaginismus
F52.6 Nonorganic dyspareunia
F52.7 Excessive sexual drive
F52.8 Other sexual dysfunction, not caused by organic disorders or disease
F52.9 Unspecified sexual dysfunction, not caused by organic disorder or disease

F53 Mental and behavioural disorders associated with the puerperium, not elsewhere classified

F53.0 Mild mental and behavioural disorders associated with the puerperium, not elsewhere classified

F53.1 Severe mental and behavioural disorders associated with the puerperium, not elsewhere classified

F53.8 Other mental and behavioural disorders associated with the puerperium, not elsewhere classified

F53.9 Puerperal mental disorder, unspecified

F54 Psychological and behavioural factors associated with disorders or diseases classified elsewhere

F55 Abuse of non-dependence-producing substances

F55.0 Antidepressants

F55.1 Laxatives

F55.2 Analgesics

F55.3 Antacids

F55.4 Vitamins

F55.5 Steroids or hormones

F55.6 Specific herbal or folk remedies

F55.8 Other substances that do not produce dependence

F55.9 Unspecified

F59 Unspecified behavioural syndromes associated with physiological disturbances and physical factors

F60 – F69
Disorders of adult personality and behaviour

F60 Specific personality disorders
F60.0 Paranoid personality disorder
F60.1 Schizoid personality disorder
F60.2 Dissocial personality disorder
F60.3 Emotionally unstable personality disorder
    .30 Impulsive type
    .31 Borderline type
F60.4 Histrionic personality disorder
F60.5 Anankastic personality disorder
F60.6 Anxious [avoidant] personality disorder
F60.7 Dependent personality disorder
F60.8 Other specific personality disorders
F60.9 Personality disorder, unspecified

F61 Mixed and other personality disorders
F61.0 Mixed personality disorders
F61.1 Troublesome personality changes

F62 Enduring personality changes, not attributable to brain damage and disease
F62.0 Enduring personality change after catastrophic experience
F62.1 Enduring personality change after psychiatric illness
F62.8 Other enduring personality changes
F62.9 Enduring personality change, unspecified

F63 Habit and impulse disorders
F63.0 Pathological gambling
F63.1 Pathological fire-setting [pyromania]
F63.2 Pathological stealing [kleptomania]
F63.3 Trichotillomania
F63.8 Other habit and impulse disorders
F63.9 Habit and impulse disorder, unspecified

F64 Gender identity disorders
F64.0 Transsexualism
F64.1 Dual-role transvestism
F64.2 Gender identity disorder of childhood

F64.8 Other gender identity disorders
F64.9 Gender identity disorder, unspecified

F65 Disorders of sexual preference
F65.0 Fetishism
F65.1 Fetishistic transvestism
F65.2 Exhibitionism
F65.3 Voyeurism
F65.4 Paedophilia
F65.5 Sadomasochism
F65.6 Multiple disorders of sexual preference
F65.8 Other disorders of sexual preference
F65.9 Disorder of sexual preference, unspecified

F66 Psychological and behavioural disorders associated with sexual development and orientation
F66.0 Sexual maturation disorder
F66.1 Egodystonic sexual orientation
F66.2 Sexual relationship disorder
F66.8 Other psychosexual development disorders
F66.9 Psychosexual development disorder, unspecified

A fifth character may be used to indicate association with:
$.x0$ Heterosexuality
$.x1$ Homosexuality
$.x2$ Bisexuality
$.x8$ Other, including prepubertal

F68 Other disorders of adult personality and behaviour
F68.0 Elaboration of physical symptoms for psychological reasons
F68.1 Intentional production or feigning of symptoms or disabilities, either physical or psychological [factitious disorder]
F68.8 Other specified disorders of adult personality and behaviour

F69 Unspecified disorder of adult personality and behaviour

F70 – F79
Mental retardation

F70 Mild mental retardation

F71 Moderate mental retardation

F72 Severe mental retardation

F73 Profound mental retardation

F78 Other mental retardation

F79 Unspecified mental retardation

A fourth character may be used to specify the extent of associated behavioural impairment:

F7x.0 No, or minimal, impairment of behaviour
F7x.1 Significant impairment of behaviour requiring attention or treatment
F7x.8 Other impairments of behaviour
F7x.9 Without mention of impairment of behaviour

F80 – F89
Disorders of psychological development

F80 Specific developmental disorders of speech and language
F80.0 Specific speech articulation disorder
F80.1 Expressive language disorder
F80.2 Receptive language disorder
F80.3 Acquired aphasia with epilepsy [Landau – Kleffner syndrome]
F80.8 Other developmental disorders of speech and language
F80.9 Developmental disorder of speech and language, unspecified

F81 Specific developmental disorders of scholastic skills
F81.0 Specific reading disorder
F81.1 Specific spelling disorder
F81.2 Specific disorder of arithmetical skills
F81.3 Mixed disorder of scholastic skills
F81.8 Other developmental disorders of scholastic skills
F81.9 Developmental disorder of scholastic skills, unspecified

F82 Specific developmental disorder of motor function

F83 Mixed specific developmental disorders

F84 Pervasive developmental disorders
F84.0 Childhood autism
F84.1 Atypical autism
F84.2 Rett's syndrome
F84.3 Other childhood disintegrative disorder
F84.4 Overactive disorder associated with mental retardation and
stereotyped movements
F84.5 Asperger's syndrome
F84.8 Other pervasive developmental disorders
F84.9 Pervasive developmental disorder, unspecified

F88 Other disorders of psychological development

F89 Unspecified disorder of psychological development

F90 – F98
Behavioural and emotional disorders with onset usually occurring in childhood and adolescence

F90 Hyperkinetic disorders
F90.0 Disturbance of activity and attention
F90.1 Hyperkinetic conduct disorder
F90.8 Other hyperkinetic disorders
F90.9 Hyperkinetic disorder, unspecified

F91 Conduct disorders
F91.0 Conduct disorder confined to the family context
F91.1 Unsocialized conduct disorder
F91.2 Socialized conduct disorder
F91.3 Oppositional defiant disorder
F91.8 Other conduct disorders
F91.9 Conduct disorder, unspecified

F92 Mixed disorders of conduct and emotions
F92.0 Depressive conduct disorder
F92.8 Other mixed disorders of conduct and emotions
F92.9 Mixed disorder of conduct and emotions, unspecified

F93 Emotional disorders with onset specific to childhood
F93.0 Separation anxiety disorder of childhood
F93.1 Phobic anxiety disorder of childhood
F93.2 Social anxiety disorder of childhood
F93.3 Sibling rivalry disorder
F93.8 Other childhood emotional disorders
F93.9 Childhood emotional disorder, unspecified

F94 Disorders of social functioning with onset specific to childhood and adolescence
F94.0 Elective mutism
F94.1 Reactive attachment disorder of childhood
F94.2 Disinhibited attachment disorder of childhood
F94.8 Other childhood disorders of social functioning
F94.9 Childhood disorders of social functioning, unspecified

F95 Tic disorders
     F95.0 Transient tic disorder
     F95.1 Chronic motor or vocal tic disorder
     F95.2 Combined vocal and multiple motor tic disorder [de la Tourette's syndrome]
     F95.8 Other tic disorders
     F95.9 Tic disorder, unspecified

F98 Other behavioural and emotional disorders with onset usually occurring in childhood and adolescence
     F98.0 Nonorganic enuresis
     F98.1 Nonorganic encopresis
     F98.2 Feeding disorder of infancy and childhood
     F98.3 Pica of infancy and childhood
     F98.4 Stereotyped movement disorders
     F98.5 Stuttering [stammering]
     F98.6 Cluttering
     F98.8 Other specified behavioural and emotional disorders with onset usually occurring in childhood and adolescence
     F98.9 Unspecified behavioural and emotional disorders with onset usually occurring in childhood and adolescence

F99
Unspecified mental disorder

F99 Mental disorder, not otherwise specified

Appendix 3

American Psychiatric Association Diagnostic and Statistical Manual III-Revised (1987) Axes I and II Categories and Codes

DSM-III-R Classification: Axes I and II Categories and Codes

All official DSM-III-R codes are included in ICD-9-CM. Codes followed by a * are used for more than one DSM-III-R diagnosis or subtype in order to maintain compatibility with ICD-9-CM.

Numbers in parentheses are page numbers.

A long dash following a diagnostic term indicates the need for a fifth digit subtype or other qualifying term.

The term *specify* following the name of some diagnostic categories indicates qualifying terms that clinicians may wish to add in parentheses after the name of the disorder.

NOS = Not Otherwise Specified

The current severity of a disorder may be specified after the diagnosis as:

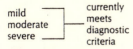

in partial remission
  (or residual state)
in complete remission

DISORDERS USUALLY FIRST EVIDENT IN INFANCY, CHILDHOOD, OR ADOLESCENCE

DEVELOPMENTAL DISORDERS
Note: These are coded on Axis II.

Mental Retardation (28)
317.00   Mild mental retardation
318.00   Moderate mental retardation
318.10   Severe mental retardation
318.20   Profound mental retardation
319.00   Unspecified mental retardation

Pervasive Developmental Disorders (33)
299.00   Autistic disorder (38)
              Specify if childhood onset
299.80   Pervasive developmental disorder NOS

Specific Developmental Disorders (39)
              Academic skills disorders
315.10   Developmental arithmetic disorder (41)
315.80   Developmental expressive writing disorder (42)
315.00   Developmental reading disorder (43)

Language and speech
disorders
315.39   Developmental articula-
            tion disorder (44)
315.31*   Developmental expres-
            sive language disorder
            (45)
315.31*   Developmental recep-
            tive language disorder
            (47)

Motor skills disorder
315.40   Developmental coordi-
            nation disorder (48)

315.90*   Specific developmental
            disorder NOS

Other Developmental Disorders
(49)
315.90*   Developmental disorder
            NOS

Disruptive Behavior Disorders (49)
314.01   Attention-deficit hyper-
            activity disorder (50)

            Conduct disorder, (53)
312.20   group type
312.00   solitary aggressive type
312.90   undifferentiated type
313.81   Oppositional defiant disorder
            (56)

**Anxiety Disorders of Childhood or
Adolescence** (58)
309.21   Separation anxiety disorder
            (58)
313.21   Avoidant disorder of child-
            hood or adolescence (61)
313.00   Overanxious disorder (63)

Eating Disorders (65)
307.10   Anorexia nervosa (65)
307.51   Bulimia nervosa (67)
307.52   Pica (69)
307.53   Rumination disorder of
            infancy (70)
307.50   Eating disorder NOS

Gender Identity Disorders (71)
302.60   Gender identity disorder of
            childhood (71)
302.50   Transsexualism (74)
            Specify sexual history:
            asexual, homosexual, het-
            erosexual, unspecified

302.85*   Gender identity disorder of
            adolescence or adulthood,
            nontranssexual type (76)
            Specify sexual history:
            asexual, homosexual, het-
            erosexual, unspecified
302.85*   Gender identity disorder
            NOS

Tic Disorders (78)
307.23   Tourette's disorder (79)
307.22   Chronic motor or vocal tic
            disorder (81)
307.21   Transient tic disorder (81)
            Specify: single episode or
            recurrent
307.20   Tic disorder NOS

Elimination Disorders (82)
307.70   Functional encopresis (82)
            Specify: primary or secon-
            dary type
307.60   Functional enuresis (84)
            Specify: primary or secon-
            dary type
            Specify: nocturnal only,
            diurnal only, nocturnal and
            diurnal

**Speech Disorders Not Elsewhere
Classified** (85)
307.00*   Cluttering (85)
307.00*   Stuttering (86)

**Other Disorders of Infancy, Childhood,
or Adolescence** (88)
313.23   Elective mutism (88)
313.82   Identity disorder (89)
313.89   Reactive attachment disorder
            of infancy or early childhood
            (91)
307.30   Stereotypy/habit disorder
            (93)
314.00   Undifferentiated attention-
            deficit disorder (95)

Appendix 3 181

ORGANIC MENTAL DISORDERS (97)

Dementias Arising in the Senium and Presenium (119)

Primary degenerative dementia of the Alzheimer type, senile onset, (119)
- 290.30 with delirium
- 290.20 with delusions
- 290.21 with depression
- 290.00* uncomplicated
  (Note: code 331.00 Alzheimer's disease on Axis III)

Code in fifth digit:
1 = with delirium, 2 = with delusions, 3 = with depression, 0* = uncomplicated

- 290.1x Primary degenerative dementia of the Alzheimer type, presenile onset, _____ (119)
  (Note: code 331.00 Alzheimer's disease on Axis III)
- 290.4x Multi-infarct dementia,_____ (121)
- 290.00* Senile dementia NOS
  Specify etiology on Axis III if known
- 290.10* Presenile dementia NOS
  Specify etiology on Axis III if known (e.g., Pick's disease, Jakob-Creutzfeldt disease)

Psychoactive Substance-Induced Organic Mental Disorders (123)

Alcohol
- 303.00 intoxication (127)
- 291.40 idiosyncratic intoxication (128)
- 291.80 Uncomplicated alcohol withdrawal (129)
- 291.00 withdrawal delirium (131)
- 291.30 hallucinosis (131)
- 291.10 amnestic disorder (133)
- 291.20 Dementia associated with alcoholism (133)

Amphetamine or similarly acting sympathomimetic
- 305.70* intoxication (134)

- 292.00* withdrawal (136)
- 292.81* delirium (136)
- 292.11* delusional disorder (137)

Caffeine
- 305.90* intoxication (138)

Cannabis
- 305.20* intoxication (139)
- 292.11* delusional disorder (140)

Cocaine
- 305.60* intoxication (141)
- 292.00* withdrawal (142)
- 292.81* delirium (143)
- 292.11* delusional disorder (143)

Hallucinogen
- 305.30* hallucinosis (144)
- 292.11* delusional disorder (146)
- 292.84* mood disorder (146)
- 292.89* Posthallucinogen perception disorder (147)

Inhalant
- 305.90* intoxication (148)

Nicotine
- 292.00* withdrawal (150)

Opioid
- 305.50* intoxication (151)
- 292.00* withdrawal (152)

Phencyclidine (PCP) or similarly acting arylcyclohexylamine
- 305.90* intoxication (154)
- 292.81* delirium (155)
- 292.11* delusional disorder (156)
- 292.84* mood disorder (156)
- 292.90* organic mental disorder NOS

Sedative, hypnotic, or anxiolytic
- 305.40* intoxication (158)
- 292.00* Uncomplicated sedative, hypnotic, or anxiolytic withdrawal (159)
- 292.00* withdrawal delirium (160)
- 292.83* amnestic disorder (161)

Other or unspecified psychoactive substance (162)
- 305.90* intoxication

292.00* withdrawal
292.81* delirium
292.82* dementia
292.83* amnestic disorder
292.11* delusional disorder
292.12   hallucinosis
292.84* mood disorder
292.89* anxiety disorder
292.89* personality disorder
292.90* organic mental disorder
         NOS

Organic Mental Disorders associated with Axis III physical disorders or conditions, or whose etiology is unknown. (162)

293.00   Delirium (100)
294.10   Dementia (103)
294.00   Amnestic disorder (108)
293.81   Organic delusional disorder (109)
293.82   Organic hallucinosis (110)
293.83   Organic mood disorder (111)
         Specify: manic, depressed, mixed
294.80* Organic anxiety disorder (113)
310.10   Organic personality disorder (114)
         Specify if explosive type
294.80* Organic mental disorder NOS

PSYCHOACTIVE SUBSTANCE USE DISORDERS (165)

         Alcohol (173)
303.90   dependence
305.00   abuse

         Amphetamine or similarly acting sympathomimetic (175)
304.40   dependence
305.70*   abuse

         Cannabis (176)
304.30   dependence
305.20*   abuse

         Cocaine (177)
304.20   dependence
305.60*   abuse

         Hallucinogen (179)
304.50*   dependence
305.30*   abuse

         Inhalant (180)
304.60   dependence
305.90*   abuse

         Nicotine (181)
305.10   dependence

         Opioid (182)
304.00   dependence
305.50*   abuse

         Phencyclidine (PCP) or similarly acting arylcyclohexylamine (183)
304.50*   dependence
305.90*   abuse

         Sedative, hypnotic, or anxiolytic (184)
304.10   dependence
305.40*   abuse

304.90* Polysubstance dependence (185)
304.90* Psychoactive substance dependence NOS
305.90* Psychoactive substance abuse NOS

SCHIZOPHRENIA (187)
Code in fifth digit: 1 = subchronic, 2 = chronic, 3 = subchronic with acute exacerbation, 4 = chronic with acute exacerbation, 5 = in remission, 0 = unspecified.

         Schizophrenia,
295.2x   catatonic, _____
295.1x   disorganized, _____
295.3x   paranoid, _____
            Specify if stable type
295.9x   undifferentiated, _____
295.6x   residual, _____
            Specify if late onset

DELUSIONAL (PARANOID) DISORDER (199)
297.10   Delusional (Paranoid) disorder

Specify type: erotomanic
grandiose
jealous
persecutory
somatic
unspecified

**PSYCHOTIC DISORDERS NOT
ELSEWHERE CLASSIFIED** (205)
298.80   Brief reactive psychosis (205)
295.40   Schizophreniform disorder
(207)
Specify: without good
prognostic features or with
good prognostic features
295.70   Schizoaffective disorder (208)
Specify: bipolar type or depressive type
297.30   Induced psychotic disorder
(210)
298.90   Psychotic disorder NOS
(Atypical psychosis) (211)

MOOD DISORDERS (213)
Code current state of Major Depression
and Bipolar Disorder in fifth digit:
1 = mild
2 = moderate
3 = severe, without psychotic
features
4 = with psychotic features (*specify*
mood-congruent or mood-
incongruent)
5 = in partial remission
6 = in full remission
0 = unspecified

For major depressive episodes, *specify*
if chronic and *specify* if melancholic
type.

For Bipolar Disorder, Bipolar Disorder
NOS, Recurrent Major Depression, and
Depressive Disorder NOS, *specify* if
seasonal pattern.

Bipolar Disorders
Bipolar disorder, (225)
296.6x   mixed, _____
296.4x   manic, _____
296.5x   depressed, _____
301.13   Cyclothymia (226)
296.70   Bipolar disorder NOS

Depressive Disorders
Major Depression, (228)
296.2x   single episode, _____
296.3x   recurrent, _____
300.40   Dysthymia (or Depressive
neurosis) (230)
Specify: primary or secondary type
Specify: early or late onset
311.00   Depressive disorder NOS

**ANXIETY DISORDERS (or Anxiety and
Phobic Neuroses)** (235)
Panic disorder (235)
300.21   with agoraphobia
Specify current severity
of agoraphobic avoid-
ance
Specify current severity
of panic attacks
300.01   without agoraphobia
Specify current severity
of panic attacks
300.22   Agoraphobia without history
of panic disorder (240)
Specify with or without limited symptom attacks
300.23   Social phobia (241)
Specify if generalized type
300.29   Simple phobia (243)
300.30   Obsessive compulsive disorder (or Obsessive compulsive
neurosis) (245)
309.89   Post-traumatic stress disorder
(247)
Specify if delayed onset
300.02   Generalized anxiety disorder
(251)
300.00   Anxiety disorder NOS

SOMATOFORM DISORDERS (255)
300.70*   Body dysmorphic disorder
(255)
300.11   Conversion disorder (or
Hysterical neurosis, conversion type) (257)
Specify: single episode or
recurrent
300.70*   Hypochondriasis (or Hypochondriacal neurosis) (259)
300.81   Somatization disorder (261)

307.80 Somatoform pain disorder
(264)
300.70* Undifferentiated somatoform
disorder (266)
300.70* Somatoform disorder NOS
(267)

**DISSOCIATIVE DISORDERS (or
Hysterical Neuroses, Dissociative Type)**
(269)
300.14 Multiple personality disorder
(269)
300.13 Psychogenic fugue (272)
300.12 Psychogenic amnesia (273)
300.60 Depersonalization disorder
(or Depersonalization neurosis) (275)
300.15 Dissociative disorder NOS

SEXUAL DISORDERS (279)

Paraphilias (279)
302.40 Exhibitionism (282)
302.81 Fetishism (282)
302.89 Frotteurism (283)
302.20 Pedophilia (284)
Specify: same sex, opposite
sex, same and opposite sex
Specify if limited to incest
Specify: exclusive type or
nonexclusive type
302.83 Sexual masochism (286)
302.84 Sexual sadism (287)
302.30 Transvestic fetishism (288)
302.82 Voyeurism (289)
302.90* Paraphilia NOS (290)

Sexual Dysfunctions (290)
Specify: psychogenic only, or psycho-
genic and biogenic (Note: If biogenic
only, code on Axis III)
Specify: lifelong or acquired
Specify: generalized or situational

Sexual desire disorders (293)
302.71 Hypoactive sexual desire
disorder
302.79 Sexual aversion disorder

Sexual arousal disorders
(294)
302.72* Female sexual arousal
disorder

302.72* Male erectile disorder

Orgasm disorders (294)
302.73 Inhibited female orgasm
302.74 Inhibited male orgasm
302.75 Premature ejaculation

Sexual pain disorders (295)
302.76 Dyspareunia
306.51 Vaginismus

302.70 Sexual dysfunction NOS

Other Sexual Disorders
302.90* Sexual disorder NOS

SLEEP DISORDERS (297)
Dyssomnias (298)
Insomnia disorder
307.42* related to another mental
disorder (nonorganic) (300)
780.50* related to known organic
factor (300)
307.42* Primary insomnia (301)
Hypersomnia disorder
307.44 related to another mental
disorder (nonorganic) (303)
780.50* related to a known organic
factor (303)
780.54 Primary hypersomnia (305)
307.45 Sleep-wake schedule
disorder (305)
Specify: advanced or de-
layed phase type,
disorganized type,
frequently changing type
Other dyssomnias
307.40* Dyssomnia NOS

Parasomnias (308)
307.47 Dream anxiety disorder
(Nightmare disorder) (308)
307.46* Sleep terror disorder (310)
307.46* Sleepwalking disorder (311)
307.40* Parasomnia NOS (313)

FACTITIOUS DISORDERS (315)
Factitious disorder
301.51 with physical symptoms
(316)
300.16 with psychological
symptoms (318)
300.19 Factitious disorder NOS (320)

Appendix 3   185

IMPULSE CONTROL DISORDERS NOT ELSEWHERE CLASSIFIED (321)
312.34 Intermittent explosive disorder (321)
312.32 Kleptomania (322)
312.31 Pathological gambling (324)
312.33 Pyromania (325)
312.39* Trichotillomania (326)
312.39* Impulse control disorder NOS (328)

ADJUSTMENT DISORDER (329)
        Adjustment disorder
309.24 with anxious mood
309.00 with depressed mood
309.30 with disturbance of conduct
309.40 with mixed disturbance of emotions and conduct
309.28 with mixed emotional features
309.82 with physical complaints
309.83 with withdrawal
309.23 with work (or academic) inhibition
309.90 Adjustment disorder NOS

PSYCHOLOGICAL FACTORS AFFECTING PHYSICAL CONDITION (333)
316.00 Psychological factors affecting physical condition
        Specify physical condition on Axis III

PERSONALITY DISORDERS (335)
Note: These are coded on Axis II.
Cluster A
301.00 Paranoid (337)
301.20 Schizoid (339)
301.22 Schizotypal (340)
Cluster B
301.70 Antisocial (342)
301.83 Borderline (346)
301.50 Histrionic (348)
301.81 Narcissistic (349)

Cluster C
301.82 Avoidant (351)
301.60 Dependent (353)
301.40 Obsessive compulsive (354)
301.84 Passive aggressive (356)
301.90 Personality disorder NOS

V CODES FOR CONDITIONS NOT ATTRIBUTABLE TO A MENTAL DISORDER THAT ARE A FOCUS OF ATTENTION OR TREATMENT (359)
V62.30 Academic problem
V71.01 Adult antisocial behavior

V40.00 Borderline intellectual functioning (Note: This is coded on Axis II.)

V71.02 Childhood or adolescent antisocial behavior
V65.20 Malingering
V61.10 Marital problem
V15.81 Noncompliance with medical treatment
V62.20 Occupational problem
V61.20 Parent–child problem
V62.81 Other interpersonal problem
V61.80 Other specified family circumstances
V62.89 Phase of life problem or other life circumstance problem
V62.82 Uncomplicated bereavement

ADDITIONAL CODES (363)
300.90 Unspecified mental disorder (nonpsychotic)
V71.09* No diagnosis or condition on Axis I
799.90* Diagnosis or condition deferred on Axis I

V71.09*	No diagnosis or condition on Axis II
799.90*	Diagnosis or condition deferred on Axis II

MULTIAXIAL SYSTEM

Axis I   Clinical Syndromes
          V Codes

Axis II   Developmental Disorders
          Personality Disorders

Axis III Physical Disorders and
          Conditions

Axis IV   Severity of Psychosocial
          Stressors

Axis V   Global Assessment of
          Functioning

Severity of Psychosocial Stressors Scale: Adults

See p. 18 for instructions on how to use this scale.

Code	Term	Examples of stressors	
		Acute events	**Enduring circumstances**
1	None	No acute events that may be relevant to the disorder	No enduring circumstances that may be relevant to the disorder
2	Mild	Broke up with boyfriend or girlfriend; started or graduated from school; child left home	Family arguments; job dissatisfaction; residence in high-crime neighborhood
3	Moderate	Marriage; marital separation; loss of job; retirement; miscarriage	Marital discord; serious financial problems; trouble with boss; being a single parent
4	Severe	Divorce; birth of first child	Unemployment; poverty
5	Extreme	Death of spouse; serious physical illness diagnosed; victim of rape	Serious chronic illness in self or child; ongoing physical or sexual abuse
6	Catastrophic	Death of child; suicide of spouse; devastating natural disaster	Captivity as hostage; concentration camp experience
0	Inadequate information, or no change in condition		

Severity of Psychosocial Stressors Scale: Children and Adolescents

See p. 18 for instructions on how to use this scale.

Code	Term	Examples of stressors	
		Acute events	**Enduring circumstances**
1	None	No acute events that may be relevant to the disorder	No enduring circumstances that may be relevant to the disorder
2	Mild	Broke up with boyfriend or girlfriend; change of school	Overcrowded living quarters; family arguments
3	Moderate	Expelled from school; birth of sibling	Chronic disabling illness in parent; chronic parental discord
4	Severe	Divorce of parents; unwanted pregnancy; arrest	Harsh or rejecting parents; chronic life-threatening illness in parent; multiple foster home placements
5	Extreme	Sexual or physical abuse; death of a parent	Recurrent sexual or physical abuse
6	Catastrophic	Death of both parents	Chronic life-threatening illness
0	Inadequate information, or no change in condition		

Appendix 3

Global Assessment of Functioning Scale (GAF Scale)

Consider psychological, social, and occupational functioning on a hypothetical continuum of mental health-illness. Do not include impairment in functioning due to physical (or environmental) limitations. See p. 20 for instructions on how to use this scale.

Note: Use intermediate codes when appropriate, e.g., 45, 68, 72.

Code

90 | 81	**Absent or minimal symptoms** (e.g., mild anxiety before an exam), **good functioning in all areas, interested and involved in a wide range of activities, socially effective, generally satisfied with life, no more than everyday problems or concerns** (e.g., an occasional argument with family members).
80 | 71	**If symptoms are present, they are transient and expectable reactions to psychosocial stressors** (e.g., difficulty concentrating after family argument); **no more than slight impairment in social, occupational, or school functioning** (e.g., temporarily falling behind in school work).
70 | 61	**Some mild symptoms** (e.g., depressed mood and mild insomnia) **OR some difficulty in social, occupational, or school functioning** (e.g., occasional truancy, or theft within the household), **but generally functioning pretty well, has some meaningful interpersonal relationships.**
60 | 51	**Moderate symptoms** (e.g., flat affect and circumstantial speech, occasional panic attacks) **OR moderate difficulty in social, occupational, or school functioning** (e.g., few friends, conflicts with co-workers).
50 | 41	**Serious symptoms** (e.g., suicidal ideation, severe obsessional rituals, frequent shoplifting) **OR any serious impairment in social, occupational, or school functioning** (e.g., no friends, unable to keep a job).
40 | 31	**Some impairment in reality testing or communication** (e.g., speech is at times illogical, obscure, or irrelevant) **OR major impairment in several areas, such as work or school, family relations, judgment, thinking, or mood** (e.g., depressed man avoids friends, neglects family, and is unable to work; child frequently beats up younger children, is defiant at home, and is failing at school).
30 | 21	**Behavior is considerably influenced by delusions or hallucinations OR serious impairment in communication or judgment** (e.g., sometimes incoherent, acts grossly inappropriately, suicidal preoccupation) **OR inability to function in almost all areas** (e.g., stays in bed all day; no job, home, or friends).
20 | 11	**Some danger of hurting self or others** (e.g., suicide attempts without clear expectation of death, frequently violent, manic excitement) **OR occasionally fails to maintain minimal personal hygiene** (e.g., smears feces) **OR gross impairment in communication** (e.g., largely incoherent or mute).
10 | 1	**Persistent danger of severely hurting self or others** (e.g., recurrent violence) **OR persistent inability to maintain minimal personal hygiene OR serious suicidal act with clear expectation of death.**

Appendix 4

Psychological Job Descriptors

It probably will never be possible to construct an exhaustive list of psychological functions. However, the following are the most commonly used by psychologists to describe the various functions that have been isolated and studied. There is often overlap between some of the terms; this should not be of concern since it reflects a difficulty psychologists sometimes have in isolating discrete functions.

GENERAL FUNCTIONS

Orientation (time, place, person, situation)	Judgment
Memory (immediate, short and long term)	Concentration
Intelligence	Writing
Reading	Follow directions
Categorize	Other

COGNITION (THINKING)

Focusing	Shifting	Concepts	Creativity
Logic	Abstract	Deductive	Other

EMOTIONS

Cheerful	Kind	Pleasant	Other

MATHEMATICS

Addition	Subtraction	Multiplication	Division
Fractions	Decimals	Ratios	Algebra
Geometry	Calculus	Trigonometry	Other

OTHER (COMBINATIONS OF FUNCTIONS)

Advise	Catalog	Classify	Compare
Coordinate	Copy	Detect	Diagnose
Edit	Estimate	Evaluate	Influence
Inspect	Instruct	Interpret	Interview
Measure	Negotiate	Observe	Organize
Plan	Read	Record	Select
Sell	Solicit	Sort	Supervise
Verify	Other		

Bibliography

Allen, R., & Loeber, R. (1972). Work assessment of psychiatric patients: A critical review of published scales. *Canadian Journal of Behavioral Science, 4*, 101–117.

American Psychiatric Association (1987). *Diagnostic and Statistical Manual III-Revised.* Washington, D.C.: Author.

Americans with Disabilities Act P.L. 101-336, 104 Stat. 327, 42 U.S.C. § 12101 et seq.

Anthony, W., & Farkas, M. (1982). A client outcome planning model for assessing psychiatric rehabilitation interventions. *Schizophrenic Bulletin, 78*: 13–38.

Anthony, W., & Jansen, M. (1984). Predicting the vocational capacity of the chronically mentally ill: Research and policy implications. *American Psychologist, 39*, 537–544.

Bidwell, G. (1969). Ego strength, self-knowledge, and vocational planning of schizophrenics. *Journal of Counseling Psychology, 16*, 45–49.

Carty v. Carlin, 623 F.Supp. 1181 (D.Md. 1985).

Chafkin, R. (1993). *Work-Site Accommodations for People with Psychiatric Disabilities.* President's Committee on Employment of People With Disabilities. 2–3.

Cheadle, J., Cushing, D., Drew, C., & Morgan, R. (1967). The measurement of the work performance of psychiatric patients. *British Journal of Psychiatry, 113*, 841–846.

Cheadle, J., & Morgan, R. (1972). The measurement of work performance by psychiatric patients: A re-appraisal. *British Journal of Psychiatry, 120,* 437–441.

Cole, N., & Shupe, D. (1970). A four-year follow-up of former psychiatric patients in industry. *Archives of General Psychiatry, 22,* 222–229.

Combs, I., & Omvig, C. (1986). Accommodation of disabled people into employment: Perceptions of employers. *Journal of Rehabilitation, 52,* 42–45.

Committee on Rating of Mental and Physical Impairment: Mental Illness. *Journal of the American Medical Association, 19(12),* 146–158.

Doe v. Region 13 Mental Health-Mental Retardation Commission, 704 F.2d 1402 (5th Cir. 1983).

Doe v. Syracuse School District, 508 F.Supp. 333 (N.D.N.Y. 1981).

Ellsworth, R., Foster, L., Childers, Arthur G., & Kroeker, D. (1968). Hospital and community adjustment as perceived by psychiatric patients, their families, and staff. *Journal of Consulting and Clinical Psychology* Monographs, 32 (3, Pt. 2).

Farina, M., & Felner, R. (1973). Employment interviewer reactions to former mental patients. *Journal of Abnormal Psychology, 82(2),* 268–272.

Fielder, J., Margiotti, M., & Taube, D. (1993). *California Institute of Psychology Modern Guide to Psychotherapy.* San Francisco: CIP Communications.

Franklin v. U.S. Postal Service, 687 F.Supp. 1214 (S.D. Ohio 1988).

Gallagher v. Catto, 778 F.Supp. 570 (D.D.C. 1991).

Gardner v. Morris, 752 F.2d 1271 (8th Cir. 1985).

Goss, A., & Pate, K. (1967). Predicting vocational rehabilitation success for psychiatric patients with psychological tests. *Psychological Reports, 21,* 725–730.

Green, H., Miskimins, R., & Keil, E. (1968). Selection of psychiatric patients for vocational rehabilitation. *Rehabilitation Counseling Bulletin, 11,* 297–302.

Guice-Mills v. Derwinski, 772 F.Supp. 188 (S.D.N.Y. 1991), 967 F.2d 794 (2d Cir. 1992).

Gurel, L., & Lorei, T. (1972). Hospital and community ratings of psychopathology as predictors of employment and readmission. *Journal of Consulting and Clinical Psychology, 34,* 286–291.

Hartlage, L., & Roland, P. (1971). Attitudes of employers toward different types of handicapped workers. *Journal of Applied Rehabilitation Counseling, 2(3),* 115–120.

Howard, G. (1975). The ex-mental patient as employee: An on-the-job evaluation. *American Journal of Orthopsychiatry, 45(3),* 479–483.

Hubbard v. U.S. Postal Service, 42 F.E.P. Cases (BNA) 1882 (D.Md. 1986).

Lorei, T. (1967). Prediction of community stay and employment for released psychiatric patients. *Journal of Consulting and Clinical Psychology, 31,* 349–357.

Lorei, T., & Gurel, L. (1973). Demographic characteristics as predictors of post-hospital employment and readmission. *Journal of Consulting and Clinical Psychology, 40,* 426–430.

Mancuso, L. (1990). Reasonable accommodation for workers with psychiatric disabilities. *Psychosocial Rehabilitation Journal, 14,* 3–19.

Massel, H., Lieberman, R., Mintz, J., Jacobs, H., Rush, T., Giannini, C., & Zarate, R. (1990). Evaluating the capacity to work of the mentally ill. *Psychiatry, 53(2),* 31–41.

Matzo v. Postmaster General, 685 F.Supp. 260 (D.D.C. 1987), 861 F.2d 1290 (D.C. Cir. 1988).

Moss, K. (1992). *Implications of Employment Complaints Filed by Persons with Mental Disabilities.* Washington, D.C.: Mental Health Policy Resource Center.

Nussbaum, K., Schneidmuhl, A., & Shaffer, J. (1969a). Psychiatric assessment in the Social Security Program of disability insurance. *American Journal of Psychiatry, 126:6,* 165–899.

Nussbaum, K., Schneidmuhl, A., & Shaffer, J. (1969b). Psychiatric disability rating in transition. *Comprehensive Psychiatry, 10,* 327–333.

Olshansky, S., Grob, S., & Malamud, I. (1958). Employers' attitudes and practices in the hiring of ex-mental patients. *Mental Hygiene, 42,* 391–401.

Pesterfield v. Tennessee Valley Authority, 941 F.2d 437 (6th Cir. 1991).

Price, L. (1965). Disability programs in the United States. *Journal of Occupational Medicine, 7,* 341–347.

Schmidt v. Bell, 33 F.E.P. Cases (BNA) 839 (E.D. Pa. 1983).

Schwartz, C., Myers, J., & Astrachan, B. (1975). Concordance of multiple assessments of the outcome of schizophrenia. *Archives of General Psychiatry, 32,* 1221–1227.

Shea v. Tisch, 870 F.2d 786 (1st Cir. 1989).

Strauss, J., & Carpenter, W. (1972). The prediction of outcome in schizophrenia. *Archives of General Psychiatry, 27,* 739–746.

Strauss, J., & Carpenter, W. (1974). The prediction of outcome in schizophrenia 2. *Archives of General Psychiatry, 31,* 37–42.

Sturm, I., & Lipton, H. (1967). Some social and vocational predictors of psychiatric hospitalization outcome. *Journal of Clinical Psychology, 23,* 301–307.

Stutts v. Freeman, 694 F.2d 666 (11th Cir. 1983).

U.S. Equal Employment Opportunity Commission & U.S. Department of Justice (1991). *Americans with Disabilities Act Handbook.* Washington, D.C.: Author.

Volle, Frank O. (1975). *Mental Evaluation of the Disability Claimant.* Springfield, Ill.: Charles C Thomas.

Wallace v. Veterans Administration, 683 F.Supp. 758 (D.Kan. 1988).

Whitlock v. Donovan, 598 F.Supp. 126 (D.D.C. 1984), 790 F.2d 964 (D.C. Cir. 1986).

Wilson, T., Berry, L., & Miskimins, W. (1969). An assessment of characteristics related to vocational success among restored psychiatric patients. *Vocational Guidance Quarterly, 18,* 110–114.

World Health Organization (1976). *International Classification of Impairments, Disabilities, and Handicaps.* Geneva: Author.

World Health Organization (1992). *ICD-10 Classification of Mental and Behavioural Disorders.* Geneva: Author.

Yandrick, R. (1993). Strategic moves. *EAPA Exchange.* August.

Index

About the Author and Contributors

JOHN F. FIELDER, Ph.D. is President and founder of the California Institute of Psychology, San Francisco. Also a consultant to the business community on ADA compliance, he has written numerous articles dealing with various topics in psychology of interest to business. He is former director of training in clinical psychology at McAuley Neropsychiatric Institute, St. Mary's Hospital and Medical Center, San Francisco, and wrote a weekly column for the *San Francisco Chronicle*.

MARIA C. BRANDT has worked at Proskauer Rose Goetz & Mendelsohn since 1986. Ms. Brandt is a member of the State Bar of California and the Bar Association of San Francisco.

JOHN H. FELDMANN III is a partner in the Labor Department of Proskauer Rose Goetz & Mendelsohn, San Francisco. Mr. Feldmann clerked for the Division of Judges of the National Labor Relations Board, 1972–73, was a field attorney for the Board's San Francisco Regional Office, 1974–75, and has practiced labor law in San Francisco since 1975. He has spoken before numerous employer groups about the Americans with Disabilities Act and has published on this topic. Mr. Feldmann is a member of the State Bar of California (Member, Labor and Employment Law Section), the State Bar of Nevada, American Bar Association (Member, Committee on Practice and Procedure Under the National Labor Relations Act, Section on Labor and Employment Law), and the Bar Association of San Francisco (Member, Labor and Employment Law Committee).